A Guide
to the
Hidden Wisdom
of Kabbalah

Third Edition

A Guide
to the
Hidden Wisdom
of Kabbalah

Third Edition

LAITMAN
KABBALAH PUBLISHERS

Rav Michael Laitman, PhD

A GUIDE TO THE HIDDEN WISDOM OF KABBALAH

Published by Laitman Kabbalah Publishers
www.kabbalah.info   info@kabbalah.info
1057 Steeles Avenue West, Suite 532, Toronto, ON, M2R 3X1, Canada
Bnei Baruch USA, 2009 85th Street #51, Brooklyn, New York, 11214, USA
Printed in Canada

Library of Congress Cataloging-in-Publication Data

Laitman, Michael.
A guide to the hidden wisdom of Kabbalah / Michael Laitman. — 3rd ed.
p. cm.
Previously published under the title: The hidden wisdom of Kabbalah.
ISBN 978-1-897448-16-8. 1. Cabala. I. Title.
BM525.L249 2009
296.1'6—dc22   2008049181

Copy Editor: Michael R. Kellog
Layout: Baruch Khovov
Cover Design: Ole Færøvik, Therese Vadem
Printing and Post Production: Uri Laitman
Executive Editor: Chaim Ratz

THIRD EDITION: OCTOBER 2009
FIRST PRINTING

CONTENTS

DETAILED
TABLE OF CONTENTS

INTRODUCTION

For many centuries, Kabbalah has been a "banned" topic. Examine this (partial) list of prerequisites you previously had to answer "yes" to in order to become a student: Jewish, male, married, over 40 years old, and proficient in other Jewish studies. So how come Kabbalah is being openly taught and studied everywhere? Because the ban has been lifted.

As Kabbalists Rav Yehuda Ashlag, the Vilna Gaon (GRA), and many other prominent Kabbalists have stated, the end of the 20ᵗʰ century marks a fundamental change in the history of Kabbalah. Now it is open for all.

As we will show inside the book, the bans were there for a reason. But it is for exactly the same reason that they have now been lifted. We, humanity in the twenty-first century, have become ready to see Kabbalah for what it really is—a scientific, time-tested, empirical method of achieving spirituality while living here in this world.

Studying Kabbalah is a fascinating journey. It changes your perspective on the world and the people around you, and opens parts in you that you never knew existed. It is a journey of discoveries happening within, affecting all of life's levels: our relationships with our kin, friends, and co-workers. Kabbalah states very simply that when you know how to connect to the Creator directly, without any go-betweens, you will find your inner compass. And this is the goal of Kabbalah—to help you make, and sustain, direct contact with the Creator. And when you do, you will need no further guidance. So welcome to *The Guide to Hidden Wisdom of Kabbalah.*

WHAT YOU'LL FIND IN THIS BOOK

The book is set up in three parts and a three part appendix. Here's what you'll find inside: Kabbalah is a science that describes the laws of the spiritual world. In Part 1, "Kabbalah Facts and Fallacies," we'll talk about the basic principles of Kabbalah and give you some background on how it began.

We'll continue our spiritual journey in Part 2, "Before there Was Time," which starts with Kabbalah's cycle of reality, explaining how we were created, what we are doing here, and how and at which point we begin our ascent to the Upper World. We'll discuss how the world was created, how Kabbalah explains what's wrong with our world today, and what needs to be done to fix it.

In this part we will also talk about how you can become a Kabbalah student and how you can use the knowledge on a day-to-day basis to your benefit. We will explain how to tell the right teacher from the wrong one, how to use books and the Internet in Kabbalah studies, and even the role of music in your spiritual progress.

Kabbalah is directly related to the state of the world today. In Part 3, "Kabbalah Today," we will explore Kabbalah's perspective of the global crises and discuss ways to cure them. Finally, we'll end with a brief tour of how Kabbalah will affect your future.

You'll also find a helpful appendix to enhance your journey and point you in the right direction if you'd like to learn more. The appendix contains a glossary, list of additional resources, and some info about our organization.

SIDEBARS

We've included five kinds of sidebars strewn throughout the text for learning and for entertainment:

Kabbalearn

Definitions of Kabbalah terms you may not be familiar with.

Tidbits

Did you know that few books about Kabbalah were written before 1980, and most were written after 2000? Check out these boxes for bits of neat stuff about Kabbalah.

Off Course

These boxes clear up misconceptions and tip you on what to avoid as you study Kabbalah.

Spiritual Sparks

Inspiring quotes and selected poems from great Kabbalists reflecting the chapter's topic of discussion.

On Course

Useful tips for putting the points in the text into practice.

I

Kabbalah
Facts
and
Fallacies

The list of celebrities studying Kabbalah reads like a who's who in Hollywood. But Kabbalah is more than a pop craze. In this section, we'll explain the popularity of Kabbalah and give an overview of what you can find if you search for Kabbalah. We'll discuss what Kabbalah is and what it isn't, and give you some background on how it started.

After reading these chapters, you'll understand why Kabbalah is becoming so trendy. You'll learn that this is not a passing fad, but an empirical science explaining the world in a way traditional sciences can't.

1

OUT IN THE OPEN

JUST THE GIST

- Kabbalah comes out of hiding
- Change is a coming
- Why now and not before
- Kabbalah and the "anything goes" spirit

The Book of Zohar, the pinnacle of Kabbalah books, writes that Kabbalah will boom and prosper at the end of days. With today's popularity of Kabbalah, it appears that the end of days is here.

Kabbalah illuminates and describes the laws of the spiritual world. It's not religion. It's a spiritual science, and for almost 2,000 years, it has been shrouded in mystery.

IN THE SPOTLIGHT

Kabbalah has traditionally been closed to all but a few select and serious students. No longer. Like never before, Kabbalah has become hot, chic, cool, in. Moreover, Kabbalists, who were previously so hesitant to open their secrets to the public, have become the key players in doing just that.

FROM SMALL GROUPS TO MASS EXPOSURE

But Kabbalah wasn't always so popular, and Kabbalists weren't nearly so open. For almost 2,000 years, Kabbalah was kept secret, shunning the public's eye for faintly lit quarters of Kabbalists who meticulously selected their students and taught them in small groups.

For instance, the 18th century Ramchal Group, the students of Rabbi Moshe Chaim Luzzato, made it especially difficult to join its ranks. Membership required agreeing to a rigorous pact of lifestyle and study that had to be met all day, every day, for as long as one remained a member.

Other groups, such as the Kotzk Group (named after a town in Poland), used to dress in worn-out clothes and treat nonmembers with offensive cynicism. They deliberately distanced themselves from others by appearing to disobey the most sacred Jewish customs like The Day of Atonement. Group members would scatter breadcrumbs on their beards to appear as if they'd been eating on this day of fasting. Naturally, most people were repelled.

Tidbits

Searching for "Kabbalah" on Amazon.com returns over five thousand books, almost none of which were written before 1980. Very few were written before 1990, and only a few more were written before the turn of the century. The vast majority of books on Kabbalah were written after the year 2000. In the last few years, Kabbalah really has been mass exposed!

Nevertheless, the same Kabbalists who hid the wisdom also made tremendous efforts to write the books that remain the pillars of Kabbalah to this day. Rabbi Isaac Luria (The Holy Ari) at once would take only one student and state that, from his time on, the study of *The Book of Zohar* (*The Zohar*, for short) is permitted to all who wish it.

For this reason, in his lifetime, the Ari taught a group of students, but at his deathbed he ordered all except Rav Chaim Vital to stop studying. The Ari said that only Chaim Vital understood the teaching properly, and he was afraid that without a proper teacher, the rest would go astray.

BREAKING THE IRON WALL

It was not until the last decade of the twentieth century that Kabbalah really began its advent to the center stage of public awareness. The single most dominant figure in the worldwide dissemination of Kabbalah is undoubtedly Rav Yehuda Ashlag, known as Baal HaSulam (Owner of the Ladder) for his *Sulam* (Ladder) commentary on *The Book of Zohar*. He was the first Kabbalist to not only speak in favor of dissemination, but to actually do it.

Baal HaSulam published a magazine, *ha-Uma* (*The Nation*), on June 5, 1940. He also tried to convince David Ben-Gurion and other leaders of the Jewish settlement in Palestine (today's Israel) to incorporate Kabbalistic principals in the education system. Baal HaSulam also stated that in the future, people of all religions would study Kabbalah while maintaining their birth religions, with no collision between the two.

> Spiritual Sparks
>
> At the outset of my words, I find a great need to break an iron wall that has been separating us from the wisdom of Kabbalah since the ruin of the Temple to this generation. It lies heavily on us and arouses fear of being forgotten.
>
> —Rav Yehuda Ashlag,
> "Introduction to the Study of the Ten Sefirot"

Such statements and the act of disseminating Kabbalah seemed so unorthodox and unacceptable at the time that *The Nation* was shut down after just one issue by the British Mandate in Palestine. In justification, the British Mandate stated that it had been told that Ashlag was promoting Communism.

KABBALAH—BECAUSE NOW WE NEED IT

Kabbalah has but a single purpose: it offers an approach that helps answer the question, "What is the meaning of my life?"

Now, more than ever before, people are asking about the meaning and the purpose of their lives. With material needs met—and met even beyond imagining, in some cases—people still feel emptiness in their lives. Kabbalah is a discipline that invokes insights and new perspectives on life, which in turn provide a spiritual fullness. This is the key to its popularity.

In *The Study of the Ten Sefirot*, an extensive commentary on the writings of the great Ari, Baal HaSulam wrote that you are ready for Kabbalah if you sometimes...

- Question the meaning of your life.
- Wonder why you and all life exist.
- Question why life can sometimes be so difficult.

THE RIGHT WISDOM FOR IT'S TIME

In the perfect cycle of life, each part has its designated function. No part of creation is free to do as it pleases because the well-being of each part depends on the well-being of all other parts of creation. Nature's law of interdependency guarantees that no creature will overpower other creatures because to destroy other creatures would mean destroying itself.

Human beings are no exception to this rule, but many—if not most—do not appreciate this idea and in one way or another act in ways that hurt others and thus themselves, as well. By controlling others or our environment, we think we can manipulate and shape the world to our liking. But a quick glimpse at the news makes you reflect on the results; all we have achieved is unhappiness for ourselves and for others. Yet, as we will show in Part 3, nothing is created without a reason, not even human destructiveness.

Today, it seems our destructiveness is causing great unhappiness to people and threatening our environment. So it shouldn't come as a surprise that people are beginning to ask questions about life that the wisdom of the Kabbalah can help us if not completely answer, at least explore more deeply.

As more people are beginning to realize that greater wealth, more sex, and additional power do not make them happier, they are no longer asking "How to?" questions, but "What for?" questions. At such a time, any doctrine that can help us answer "What for?" questions has a good chance at popularity.

Because Kabbalah specifically explores questions about the meaning of life, it's not surprising many people find it appealing. This, coupled with the publicity generated by its celebrity adherents, has brought it to the attention of seekers everywhere.

KABBALAH WITH ANYTHING

In the "anything goes" spirit of today's world, everything's mixed with everything else: science with religion, rock and roll with Beethoven. There is even sushi ice cream (bet you didn't know that). Following the trend, Kabbalah has been associated with more doctrines and teachings than there are toppings for pizza.

But there is another, more serious reason for the sudden emergence of this ancient discipline. Kabbalah has always had a reputation of possessing insight into the highest forces of nature, of the spiritual worlds, and of the nature of God. As a result, people have always wanted to connect Kabbalistic terms with all kinds of teachings.

The problem with such connections is that they undermine the power of Kabbalah to help us understand our human and spiritual natures. This, after all, is at the heart of today's interest in this teaching, and the reason Kabbalah was developed in the first place.

So, to clear up any misconceptions, let's look at what Kabbalah is not. It is not, and has nothing to do with religion, magic, mysticism, divination, cults, holistic medicine, meditation, philosophy, theosophy, psychology or parapsychology, ESP, telepathy, dream interpretation, tarot cards, yoga, red strings, holy water, blessings, past-life regressions, numerology, reiki, channeling, astrology, astral travels or projection, communicating with the dead, out-of-body experiences, voodoo, freemasonry, reflexology, UFO's, creationism, Sufism or any ism.

Kabbalah has been around for a long, long time and is only now taking its place in the general public awareness. Those who embrace it as the latest fad will perhaps move on to something else. But those who dig deeply into its principles are likely to find enough to keep them going for a lifetime.

IN A NUTSHELL
- Kabbalah is a method that answers life's deepest question: "What is the meaning of my life?"
- Kabbalah has been waiting in hiding until the questions it answers arose.
- Kabbalah has been incorrectly associated with many flavors of spiritual teachings.
- Kabbalah is not a passing fad, but a time-tested, practical method to understanding human nature and the nature of the Creator.

2

Some Basics

JUST THE GIST

- The real reality
- The door to the "sixth sense" opens
- Getting to know what we want
- At the heart of selfishness lies true giving

Now that we've cleared up common misconceptions about Kabbalah, let's see what it's really all about. This chapter briefly presents the basic concepts of Kabbalah. The terms we present and discuss in this chapter set up the language of Kabbalah that we use throughout the book.

This chapter also presents how and why your study of Kabbalah is not only good for you, but also for the benefit of society as a whole.

THE TRUTH ABOUT REALITY

In Hebrew, the word *Kabbalah* means "reception." But Kabbalah isn't just that—reception. It's a discipline of study, a method that teaches you *how* to receive. Kabbalah helps you know where you truly are in relation to where you think you are. It shows the boundaries of our five senses and opens up the part that they can't reveal by helping you develop a "sixth sense."

This sixth sense not only enriches your life with a new dimension, but opens a door to a "brave new world." There is no death in this world, no sorrow, no pain. And best of all, you don't have to give up anything for it: you don't have to die to get there; you don't have to fast or restrain yourself in any way. In short, Kabbalah

Kabbalearn

In his essay "The Essence of the Wisdom of Kabbalah," Baal HaSulam defines Kabbalah as follows: "This wisdom is no more and no less than a sequence of roots, which hang down by way of cause and consequence in fixed, determined rules, interweaving to a single, exalted goal described as 'the revelation of His Godliness to His creatures in this world.'"

doesn't take you away from life; it adds a whole new meaning and strength to everything that happens. That's right, Kabbalists live life to the fullest.

TO RECEIVE—DISCOVER THE FORCE OF GIVING

To understand the kind of pleasure that the Kabbalist receives, it's essential to understand a basic concept in Kabbalah: In the whole of reality, there is only a single force—the force of giving. And because that force is giving, it creates "something" to receive what it gives. The giving force in Kabbalah is called "Creator," and what it creates is called "creation," a "creature" or a "created being." The created being is us, humanity as a whole and each of us in person.

This creature goes through a process of learning and development, and at its end discovers the full grandeur and beauty of its Creator. Baal HaSulam explains that this revelation of the Creator to the creature is the essence and the purpose of the whole of creation.

REALITY AS AN EMBROIDERY

Now let's talk a little more about revealing the Creator. When Baal HaSulam describes the purpose of Kabbalah as "the revelation of His Godliness to His creatures in this world," he means that the essence of Kabbalah ("reception") is to discover the Creator because this is what gives us the ultimate pleasure.

But there is more to it: Kabbalah explains that discovering the Creator means discovering the law that governs nature. In fact, the Creator is nature. By disclosing this law of nature, Kabbalah aims to disclose reality in its entirety, the whole gamut, revealing why things happen to us and how we can not only predict them, but change them to our benefit.

Also, if you can understand all sides of nature, you can reach far beyond your present physical life, far beyond the boundaries of your five senses, as if someone has removed a blindfold from your eyes and allowed you to see the true vastness and beauty of the world.

How does it work, and what do you actually receive? Reality is like embroidery. When you look at an embroidery you see a coherent picture. But when you look behind the picture, at the threads that make up the picture, you find a mess of strings and cords that you can't decide where they begin, where they end, and which part of the picture they belong to. Kabbalah helps you understand the threads behind the picture of reality, and teaches you how to become an embroiderer yourself, so you can build a picture that suits your liking.

THE LATENT SENSE

Reception in Kabbalah is all about perceiving the spiritual world. It is a world invisible to the five senses, but one we certainly experience. If everything we perceive depends on our senses, it stands to reason that all we need to sense the spiritual world is a special sense that perceives it. In other words, we don't need to look for anything outside of us, but we need to cultivate a perception that already exists within us that lies dormant. In Kabbalah, this perception is called "the sixth sense."

Actually, the title, "sixth sense," is a bit misleading; it is not a "sense" in the physiological meaning of the word. But because it enables us to perceive something that we otherwise wouldn't, Kabbalists have decided to call this different means of perception "the sixth sense."

Here's the crux of it all: our five senses are "programmed" to serve personal interests. For this reason, all we perceive is what seems to serve our best interests. If your senses were somehow programmed to serve the interest of the whole world, then that's what we would perceive. In this way, each of us would be able to perceive what every other person, animal, plant, or mineral in the universe perceives. We would become creatures of unlimited perception—omniscient, literally Godlike people.

> **Kabbalearn**
>
> In Hebrew, the name "Adam" comes from the word *Domeh*, as in *Dome la Elyon* (similar to the Upper One), as described in the verse, "I will be like the Most High" (Isaiah 14:14).

In such an unbounded state, the five senses would be used in a very different way. Instead of focusing on personal interests, they would serve as means of communication with others. This is why the sixth sense, which enables perception of the spiritual worlds, is not a sense in the usual meaning of the word; it is the intention with which we use our senses. Intention is a critical Kabbalah concept that we explore more fully in Chapter 4.

THE CREATOR HAS TO GIVE; WE HAVE TO RECEIVE

Kabbalah is really very simple, once you know it. It explains that the Creator is benevolent and that He wants to give us endless, infinite pleasure. Because the Creator is benevolent, He created us with an endless, infinite desire to receive the pleasure He wants to give. In Kabbalah, this is called "the will to receive delight and pleasure," or, in short, "the will to receive."

On Course

Basically, intention is the "goal" for which we act. If we want to benefit ourselves, then all we see is ourselves and all that we have created. But if we want to benefit the Creator, then all we'll see will be the Creator's world and all that He has created.

In his "Introduction to the Book of Zohar," Baal HaSulam explains the Creator's necessity to create the will to receive (creatures):

> Since the Thought of Creation was to bestow upon His creatures, He had to create in the souls a great measure of desire to receive that which He had thought to give them. ...Thus, the Thought of Creation itself necessarily dictates the creation of an excessive will to receive in the souls, to fit the immense pleasure that His Almightiness thought to bestow upon the souls.

In other words, we have the capability, potential, and even unconscious desire to connect with the Creator and, in receiving His pleasures, enhance our joy in living.

SELFISH TO THE CORE

But in practice, there are consequences to such an immense will to receive. Baal HaSulam himself describes the complexity of the human condition in his essay "Peace in the World":

> each and every individual feels himself in the world of the Creator, as a sole ruler, that all the others were created

only to ease and improve his life, without him feeling any
obligation whatsoever to give anything in return.

In plain words, we're selfish to the core. However, when
corrected, this extreme egoism becomes the highest level of
altruism and benevolence.

THE MOST EGOISTIC DESIRE: TO BE AN ALTRUIST

But being born selfish doesn't mean we will remain selfish forever.
Remember that the Creator is benevolent; He has nothing on
His mind but giving. As a result, He creates creatures that want
only to receive. These creatures begin to receive what He gives,
more, and more, and more. Endlessly.

As the will to receive evolves in creatures, an almost magical
transformation takes place. They not only want what the Creator
gives, but they also want to actually *be* Creators. Think of how every child wants to become like his or her parents. Think, too, how
the very basis of learning is
the little one's desire to grow.
Kabbalists say the child's will
to be a grown up stems from
the creature's desire to be like
its Creator.

Spiritual Sparks

There is a wonderful, invaluable
remedy to those who engage in the wisdom
of Kabbalah .... [T]hey awaken upon themselves the Lights that surround their souls ....
[T]he illumination received time-after-time
during the study draws upon one grace
from Above, imparting abundance of sanctity and purity, which bring one much closer
to perfection.

—Baal HaSulam,

"Introduction to the Study of the Ten Sefirot"

If your parents are your
role models, you would
study their actions and do
your best to emulate them
and become a grownup, too.
Similarly, if the Creator is
your role model, you would study the Creator in order to become like Him. If the Creator you study is all about giving, about
benevolence, you can see how the extreme egoism of wanting
to become "Creatorlike" can be turned into altruism (which we

explore more fully in upcoming chapters), because that's what He is. In Kabbalah, the ability to be like the Creator is called "achieving the attribute of bestowal."

The implication, though it may sound like an oxymoron, is that every person's *most egoistic desire* is to be like the Creator: a total altruist.

> **On Course**
>
> Another way to think about this idea of altruism is to remember that Kabbalah reminds us that we are not separate from but part of our world. Altruism is about being one with others, united with them. From this perspective, altruism is an intelligent way to look out for our own welfare, as well.

IN A NUTSHELL
- Kabbalah provides a method by which you learn to receive.
- The Creator's primary desire is to give pleasure, so He imbues His creations with a desire to receive that pleasure.
- The "sixth sense" allows you to perceive higher spiritual worlds.
- The purpose of Kabbalah is the revelation of the Creator while we are living here in this world.
- The biggest egoists want to be like the Creator: altruists.

3

REALITY CHECK

JUST THE GIST
- Reality—not what meets the eye
- The boundaries of our subjective perception
- We are made of four factors (layers), and we can change one, to change all
- Free choice really isn't free, except the choice in the environment

Now that we have a basic understanding of how Kabbalah developed and what it is, it's time to take a deeper look at what Kabbalah does for you. This chapter expands upon the concepts introduced in Chapter 2, in order to show how Kabbalists understand the Creator and what the Creator wishes for you.

This chapter also explores more fully the nature of reality and what you perceive and don't perceive about reality. You also learn more about the power of free choice and how to focus your mind on what helps you change your life for the better.

IS THIS ALL THERE IS?

Look around you. What do you see? What do you hear? Have you ever wondered if there's anything out there that your five senses can't detect? Perhaps other worlds and creatures exist within the space you can't perceive—worlds that are transparent and unrecognizable from our point of view?

To a Kabbalist, we are living in darkness, unable to see the greater reality, although it is still there. Without knowing any better we take this view of the world as the only possible reality. But think of Kabbalah as a way of illuminating the *whole* of reality so that it is plain to see. Once that happens and we take it all in, our perceptions of reality are changed. We can no longer act the way we did when we were in the dark, and this is to the mutual benefit of ourselves and of others.

> **Spiritual Sparks**
>
> Our five senses and our imagination offer us nothing more than the disclosure of the actions of the Essence, but not the Essence itself. For example, the sense of sight offers us only shadows of the visible Essence, according to how they are formed opposite the Light.
>
> —Rav Yehuda Ashlag, "Preface to the Book of Zohar"

BEYOND THE FIVE SENSES

Do you ever think that your hand feels odd because you have only five fingers? Probably not. Although we can increase the range our five senses perceive, we cannot really imagine what perceptions we lack. It's impossible to recognize the true reality because it isn't something that we feel the absence of any more than we feel the lack of a sixth finger.

Because imagination is the product of the five senses, we can never envision an object or creature that is not in some way already familiar. Think of the most creative children's book illustrator or the most abstract artist you know. Do their designs in some way resemble things that exist in the physical world? Try to imagine the wildest thing, and you will still create something already known or that you can puzzle out from your experience of everyday reality.

Going beyond the five senses doesn't happen literally. It's more of a way to describe a higher level of perception where we understand the interconnectedness of everything and our place in this interconnected reality.

Quite possibly, you and I receive many sensations from external objects. But because our senses do not have the same qualities as those objects, we do not perceive them. We perceive only that part of the object that resonates to qualities we already have. For a complete perception of anything, we need to first be complete within. In other words, we have to be aware of all the forms of reality that exist in us, and then our picture of reality will be complete.

> **Spiritual Sparks**
>
> You must therefore understand and perceive that all the names and appellations, and all the worlds, Upper and lower, are all one Simple Light, Unique and Unified. In the Creator, the spreading Light, the Thought, the Operation, the Operator, and anything the heart can think and contemplate are one and the same thing.
>
> —Rav Yehuda Ashlag, The Study of the Ten Sefirot

So how do we attain the sixth sense that enhances our perception beyond conventional reality? In fact, it exists in everyone but is hidden. Remember the intention mentioned in the previous chapter? With it, we can bring this dormant sense into action.

Through persistence and study, we begin to gain perception of the world of the Creator—the world of giving. In Kabbalah, that world is called "the Upper World." By study and development of the sixth sense, we gradually begin to feel and to understand the Upper World.

ACROSS THE BARRIER

Our perception of the Upper World varies depending on our spiritual state. Initially, we cannot perceive the Upper World because our qualities are opposite from the Creator's. In such a state, we can only perceive the material world we presently live in, and everything we imagine the spiritual world to be is strictly a figment of our imagination.

But once we acquire the first spiritual quality, the first bit of altruism, we also gain the ability to see the spiritual as it truly is. Kabbalists call it "crossing the barrier." Once we cross the barrier we can advance even without a teacher because in that state we are under the conscious guidance of the Creator. Still, in most cases, Kabbalists continue to study with a teacher even after they cross the barrier, but their relationship with their teacher changes drastically: the teacher no longer needs to lead a blind person by the hand, but the two walk together on an enchanted path of discovery.

Beyond the barrier, one learns from one's own soul, through observation of the soul and its relationship with the Creator. To understand this learning process, think of how we hear. The hearing mechanism reacts to some pressure from the outside by working in the same way as the pressure but in the opposite direction, pressing back from within. This way, it keeps itself in balance, enabling you to measure, in this case, the volume and pitch of a sound. But here's the hitch: for this type of perception to occur, there must be some uniting element between the perceiver and the object of perception. In the case of our hearing it's the eardrum.

But what's the uniting force that can tie our perception to the Creator? Perhaps what we need is a "spiritual eardrum," which would have the same quality as what's given out by the Creator? Well, such an "eardrum" exists; it is the intention introduced in Chapter 2. Whatever you do with an *intention* to give is considered "giving" in spirituality. The problem is to see where your intention is to receive and turn it into an intention to give. More on how this is done in Chapter 12: Studying Kabbalah.

THE ONLY REALITY IS WITHIN

Our understanding of what we sense is based on the genes we inherit, our experiences, our socialization, and what we have learned. It's all totally subjective. Regardless of what our senses take in, what we eventually understand of it and how we act as a result are very personal.

For example, if we were deaf, wouldn't there still be sounds around us? Wouldn't there still be music and the sound of jet planes roaring over our heads? Would birds stop singing because we wouldn't be able to hear them? To us, they would. There is no way to explain to a deaf person what a nightingale sounds like. Moreover, no two people experience the same experience when they hear the same sound.

All that you and I believe to exist outside of us are actually experiences we sense within us. We have no way of telling what they are truly like in and of themselves. So when we think of reality, we are actually thinking of what *we* view as objective through the lens of our own perception.

IN SEARCH OF FREEDOM

Let's begin this section with an allegory by Baal HaSulam: Once there was a king who wanted to know which of his subjects were trustworthy. He announced that anyone who wanted to come and work for him would be handsomely rewarded by a festive meal, fit for kings. When the people arrived, there was no one at the gate, just a sign indicating where to go and what to do, but no guards to watch over the arrivals. Those who worked in the designated area were unknowingly exposed to a magic powder, and those who went elsewhere were not. In the evening, when everyone sat at the table, those who worked where the sign indicated enjoyed the meal tremendously, but to those who didn't, the food was the worst they'd ever tasted. Thus, only those who freely chose to follow the king were rewarded with enjoying what the king enjoys.

It has long been said that people are only truly happy if they are truly free—free from bondage, free from oppression, and free to make their own decisions. Likewise, people have long wondered how to reconcile the concept of free will with the existence of a greater power, and in the case of Kabbalists—the Creator.

The Creator's singular desire is for you and me to be fulfilled and made joyful. This state can occur only when we reach His state, His degree. This can happen only when our desire to enjoy is equal to the Creator's desire to bestow enjoyment. If it sounds circular, it is: it's the reciprocity that brings us ever closer to perfection and the Creator's wish for us. So how do we reconcile this idea of free will with what the Creator wishes for us?

Here's the Kabbalist's logic, step by step:

1. The Creator is absolutely benevolent.
2. As a result, He wants to grant us absolute pleasure.
3. Absolute pleasure means being in His state: omniscient, omnipotent, and benevolent.
4. Therefore, we have to come to feel that His state is the absolute good state. In other words, we have to *choose* it of our own free will.
5. Free choice can only be made on condition that the Creator does not apply force on us, so that we are independent from Him.
6. Therefore, He is hidden and gave us the existence in this world where we don't sense the Creator as vividly and as tangibly as we sense physical objects.

7. Without feeling Him as either fearsome or good, but from a completely "neutral" state, we could decide freely that being like Him is the absolute good.

FAKE FREEDOM

Kabbalah teaches that even though the Creator wants to enter into a relationship with His creation, He has concealed Himself from us to give the impression of free will. Under these conditions, we seem to be able to act, think, and choose, completely independent of the Creator's presence. Our choices appear to be made of our own volition and free will; we do not detect an unseen hand guiding our actions and, as far as we can tell, our choices are truly free.

Think of it this way: the Creator has your entire life planned out for you, down to what you will have for lunch today. But if the Creator has all of our decisions and moves mapped out in advance, is free choice truly free? The answer is that our choices are free when looking from our perspective. The fact that the Creator knows what we will decide is meaningless to us, as long as *we* don't know what we will choose.

THE PLEASURE AND PAIN PRINCIPLE

As we just explained, the Creator's only wish is for us to be filled with joy. Recognizing this truth is central to our path to perfection. It is no secret that we all desire pleasure and often go to great lengths to find it.

But if the Creator's intent was for us to seek and experience endless pleasure, how does pain fit into the equation? You and I do not commit to any action unless we believe that it will, in some way, make us feel good or, at least, better. Each of our actions is a result of a calculation that our happiness will increase. In this way, you and I consciously put ourselves through painful situations to gain greater pleasure.

Certain painful situations make us reevaluate what we believe are the causes of our happiness and rank them according to importance. Say you have a Rolex watch, the ownership of which brings you great pleasure—what it represents in the way of achievement, what it says about your status, and who knows what else. One day, a mugger puts a gun to your chest and demands your beloved watch, or else... Most sane people would agree to a painful act (in this case, giving up a cherished item) in order to avoid a more painful act (injury of some sort or worse).

>
> ### Spiritual Sparks
> The living creatures have no freedom... to choose pain or reject pleasure. And man's advantage over animals is that he can aim at a remote goal, to agree to a certain amount of current pain, out of choice of future benefit or pleasure, to be attained after some time.
>
> ...And so it sometimes happens that we are tormented because we did not find the attained pleasure to be the surplus... compared to the agony we suffered; hence, we are in deficit, just as merchants do.
>
> --Baal HaSulam, "The Freedom"

Think of it as a sort of pleasure-ranking system. People can calculate that any current discomfort is worth the future pleasure. In other words, current pain may be worthwhile in order to obtain some future pleasure.

FOUR FACTORS (LAYERS) OF OUR MAKEUP

Kabbalah states that four factors determine a person's state at each and every moment:

1. **Source**. This is the starting point, the spiritual gene-pool. But it is not a blank canvas. Think of it more as a wall that has been painted and repainted many times. The layers of previous coats of paint are there beneath the surface. Perhaps they cannot be seen or distinguished, but they are a part of the composition of that wall, always the starting point for the next

layer of transformation, as a wall's current paint is always the undercoat for the next coat.

2. **Unchanging paths of development that stem from one's nature.** This factor deals with the way we evolve as a result of our genes. These paths may refer to things we tend to like or dislike, our talents and other hereditary traits.

3. **Paths of development that change under the influence of external factors.** This is our attitude toward the external environment. Say you get a bad performance review from your boss at work. You may be upset and angry, and feel that the feedback is unfair, or you may decide your boss has your best interest at heart and told you what you need to do in order to succeed. Either way, the external event of your boss' criticism will inevitably affect you and change you.

On Course

Why does your attitude, whatever it is, change the environment? The answer is that you are not separate from but another part of the environment. Given this, an important question to ask would be "What attitude should I adopt so as to make my environment better?"

4. **Paths of development of the external factors themselves.** The fourth factor is the external environment and its continued evolution. To continue the previous example, if you chose to change your boss (perhaps by changing your job), this would expose you to a new set of influences, but these would be influences you have *chosen* to be under.

As the four factors show, the confluence of a person's origin, inner nature, unchangeable and changeable outside forces all contribute to our inner makeup. However, of all four elements, the only element we can modify is the fourth, our environment. But because the elements affect each other, by changing our environment, we can ultimately shape all other elements within us.

IN A NUTSHELL

- What we perceive as our world is a subjective image of what the Creator has really given to us.
- The Creator wants only to give to you, and as you receive, you will want to be like the Creator and give back to Him.
- Four factors determine your state at any moment: Source, unchanging paths of development that stem from one's nature, paths of development that change under the influence of external factors, and paths of development of the external factors themselves.
- If you want to change your desires and direction in life, you must take control over the environment you live in.

4

THE HISTORY OF DESIRES

JUST THE GIST
- Five levels of desire
- Recognition of evil as a condition for discovering the Creator
- The "point in the heart"
- Intention is life's decisive force

The history of humankind runs on a par with the story of human desires and how they developed. The search for ways of fulfilling our desires determines the speed and direction of a civilization's evolution and defines how it measures progress.

This chapter explores the development of human desires, from basic needs all the way up to the highest level: the need for spirituality. You can begin a serious study of Kabbalah only after you've acquired that need; it is the gateway to understanding the Creator's role and our own role in the world.

FIVE LEVELS OF DESIRES

The list of humankind's achievements is parallel to a list of its desires. Humans' desire to transfer more goods at a faster pace prompted the invention of the wheel. And humans' desire to rule and conquer was the driving force behind the invention of the canon in the Middle Ages.

As collective desires grow, civilizations advance. Kabbalah divides the entire complex of human desires into five levels:

Level 1. Meeting basic natural desires, such as food, shelter, and sex

Level 2. Striving for wealth

Level 3. Craving power and fame

Level 4. Thirsting for knowledge

Level 5. Desiring spirituality

Once the immediate craving is fulfilled, however, a feeling of "emptiness" appears. The more the process repeats itself, the more a person is driven to question the profitability of the empty-full-empty process itself. Once we give up on finding fulfillment to our desires on one level, we try the same in the next. And when desires of the first four levels have all proven incapable of providing lasting fulfillment, we begin to ask, "Is there anything more to life than chasing material goods and social status?" When that happens, we begin to want spirituality. In Kabbalah, this state is called "the appearance of the point in the heart" (More on that below in this chapter).

THE RECOGNITION OF EVIL AND THE REVELATION OF GOOD

In the previous chapter, we talked about the recognition of evil, that is, the recognition that we are egoists, acting only in our own interest. We said that if we consider our state as totally evil, and His state as utterly desirable, we will cross the barrier and enter the spiritual world. The question that remains open is which is the quickest and most painless way to recognize our evil. This is where Kabbalah comes into play. The advantage in Kabbalah is that it teaches you about human nature without having to physically experience the evil. This is why Kabbalists say we don't have to suffer; we can study instead.

Kabbalearn

In Kabbalah, correct refers to correction. No one will tell you that who you are or what you do is correct or incorrect. But if you've used a desire to become more "Creatorlike," then you've done the correct thing. To Kabbalists, correction means turning the intention with which we use a desire from "for me" to "for the Creator."

In that sense, humans finish the Creator's creation, meaning that they *correct* it. Because humans have the ability to be like the Creator, the Creator passes on to them the leadership of creation, once they are corrected. So the good purpose of evil is realized only if egoism becomes a driving force towards the Creator. Otherwise, evil is evil is evil. And it produces evil, as egoistic acts throughout history show.

The Creator increases the pressure on us to make us take control of ourselves. This is why the world seems to become increasingly hostile. The Creator made it that way so you and I would begin to correct the world and ourselves. If He hadn't done it this way, you and I would sit under a tree and work on our tan. Although that may sound great, it doesn't bring you any closer to becoming like the Creator, which is why He created us in the first place.

The Creator wants us to partake in our own creation. If you remember that, all your calculations stop being passive. Instead, they become tools with which you contact the Creator and experience Him. Every negative, or evil, attribute in you becomes a means to an end.

In Kabbalah, there is no other way to make contact with the Creator—only through realization that our attributes are negative. Put differently, the recognition of evil is the beginning of the revelation of good.

This explanation of the Creator's goal leaves one question open: if he wants to give us pleasure, as Kabbalists say, what's wrong with a good tan, if we enjoy it? Well, there is nothing wrong with it, if that's what you really want. But if you have a question nagging in the back of your mind (while lying on the beach), and you can't enjoy sunbathing anymore, then maybe you need something more, and maybe that something is Kabbalah. As Baal HaSulam puts it: Kabbalah is for those who ask (even unconsciously), "What is the meaning of my life?"

FEELING GOOD, THEN BETTER

Behind all our desires is the search for satisfaction. Kabbalah explains that life is based on only one desire: to feel good, regardless of whether that good feeling comes through obtaining a better job, a new car, a mate, or successful children.

When you begin to feel spirituality, it changes your scale of desire. You may begin to see that some desires have become more important and others have become less so. You begin to weigh your life not according to what you see and know in this world, what your physical body sees right now, but according to a much broader scale. You begin to see what favors you and what does not for generations to come. As a result, you change how you assess your environment.

When you begin to realize that you are a part of a single soul and that all of humanity are parts of that soul, too, you begin to think that it may be in your interest to help them. In short, Kabbalah reminds you to look at the big picture.

Ironically, however, the more you want spirituality, the more you want mundane pleasures, too. A Kabbalist is not a person without desires for food, sex, money, power, and knowledge. On the contrary, a Kabbalist is one with stronger mundane desires than most people experience, but also with a desire for spirituality that is greater than all his or her mundane desires put together.

This process of intensifying is designed to make you develop such a strong desire for spirituality that you will be willing to do anything to attain it, including conceding all desires that are not for spirituality. But to give up those desires, you must experience them. This is why Kabbalists explain that the higher your spiritual degree, the greater your mundane desires, too. Kabbalists progress by experiencing the greatest worldly pleasures, and then being given the awareness that there is something that's even better and greater than all those pleasures combined.

In spirituality, just as in our world, your desires change as you grow. The earlier objects of your desire seem like toys compared to the things you seek now. That search finally leads to the absolute good—direct contact with the Creator, achieved through equivalence of form with Him, through being like Him.

A WIN, WIN SITUATION

But if the Creator made a world in order to bestow His abundance to the created beings, then what's wrong with wanting to receive everything "for oneself"? Why is it perceived as evil or egoism? Why was it necessary to create a world so imperfect and a creation so corrupted that it must be corrected?

Kabbalists explain that the Creator receives pleasure by giving pleasure to His created beings—us. If we delight in the fact that our reception pleases the Creator, then the Creator and we coincide in qualities and in desires. In this way, everyone thinks of the other, not of him or herself, and everyone still receives pleasure; it's a win, win situation.

WHEN SEX, POWER, AND KNOWLEDGE DON'T DO IT FOR ME

When desires for worldly pleasures—food, sex, family, wealth, power, and knowledge—fail to keep their promise of lasting happiness, "the point in the heart" begins to develop. It's a desire for something higher, appearing when all the mundane desires have exhausted themselves.

Kabbalearn

Kabbalah distinguishes the desire for the Creator from all other desires. Desires for worldly pleasures are called "man's heart," while the desire for the Creator is called "the point in the heart."

THE POINT IN THE HEART

The point in the heart, the desire for Light—the Creator—awakens within the egoistic desires, which an individual cannot fulfill. Faced with the inability to satisfy the desire for the Creator through worldly means, a person comes to the final state of the evolution of the will to receive.

When that happens, that person often feels dark inside. But this is not because he or she has grown worse. On the contrary, it is because that person has become more corrected, drawn more Light, and the new Light shines on new places in the soul. But because these places are not yet corrected, they often give off a "dark" feeling. When darkness appears, it's a sure sign that you have made progress and that Light is sure to follow.

In the "Introduction to the Study of the Ten Sefirot," Baal HaSulam writes that it's as if the Creator appears to a person from amidst the cracks in a wall and offers hope for future peace. In Kabbalah, this is called "putting one's hand on the good fortune."

ZOOMING ON THE "WHY"

The real work begins once the point in the heart opens up. In Kabbalah, the focal point is the *intention*. Desires create our thoughts, but intentions give them direction. This, in turn, creates our actions and ultimately our whole reality.

Spiritual Sparks

For man looks on the outward appearance, but the Lord looks on the heart.

—Samuel 1, 16:7

Using the study of Kabbalah, you can concentrate on developing intentions that affect reality in a way that elevates you to experience the Upper World, the Creator.

In the science of Kabbalah, the thought is the intention, because it is its progenitor. In a regular life, thought is the considerations made by the desire to receive. The desire to receive in and of itself isn't bad—that's how you and I were created, and when used correctly it is beneficial to us and to the Creator. The intention in which we use our desire is where we must focus our attention.

In simple words, we must become aware of *why* we do what we do, what we want to get out of it, and whom we want to please by experiencing pleasure—ourselves or the Creator. This intention will then create a work plan, a thought, and the thoughts will determine our whole reality. So the only part that needs mending in reality is our intentions. That's why Kabbalists say that what you do doesn't matter, only what you aim to achieve by it. The following section will elaborate on that.

COUPLING WITH THE CREATOR

The intent of the Creator from the start was to make the desire complete. However, this happens only when your intent resembles the Creator's attribute of bestowal by your free choice. This requires transforming your will for self-enjoyment into the will to please the Creator. And the Creator is pleased when you acquire His qualities.

When you acquire this intent, the desire to enjoy becomes equal to the Creator's desire to give. You bring yourself to perfection by the correct use of your only attribute: the reception of pleasure. This is a change in intent, a change in the aim of your actions and not your actions themselves. Changing the intent of one's desire involves three phases:

1. Avoiding the use of desire in its original form.
2. Isolating from your desire to enjoy only those desires that you can use in order to please the Creator.
3. Correcting the intention of the worthy desires and achieving sameness with the Creator in those desires. In Kabbalah, this is called "coupling with the Creator" or discovering the Creator."

In spirituality, you turn away from looking at the picture of reality you are born with. Instead, you get to know the forces that paint the picture. You get to know the artist. You acquire the ability to connect to the forces that create the picture, and ultimately to govern those forces. You begin to understand how reality is made.

This goes for society as a whole as well as for individuals. Today, many among us have already completed Levels 1-4 and are now embarking on Level 5, the spiritual level. This is a time when people will want to know what they are living for. Our next chapter will explore key points in the evolution of Kabbalah and their congruence with the history of humanity.

IN A NUTSHELL

- There are five levels of desire: food and sex, wealth, power, knowledge, and spirituality. The only one we can really fulfill is the last.

- History is really a tale of heightening, insatiable desires.
- Your negative attributes will eventually lead you to know the Creator.
- The desire for more worldly things necessarily leads to greater emptiness because our true (unconscious desire) is to know the Creator.
- Intention is the force that drives the outcome of actions, the aim behind the act.

5

KABBALAH—ITS HISTORY AND VIPS

JUST THE GIST
- Reality evolved from thought to matter, to man.
- Adam and *The Angel of God's Secret*
- Abraham and *The Book of Creation*
- Moses and *The Torah*
- Shimon Bar Yochai and *The Book of Zohar*
- The Ari and *The Tree of Life*

Kabbalah doesn't talk about the physical existence of the universe, but what it says about spirituality has a corresponding part in the physical world. In this chapter, you learn about the history of Kabbalah and the people who contributed to its position as a key player in the human drama.

FROM THE FIRST THOUGHT TO THE FIRST MAN

The history of Kabbalah corresponds to the history of creation. The Thought of Creation caused creation to happen. The Thought of Creation is called the Root Phase or Phase Zero. Phase Zero generated four more phases, which then generated a Root World, which is still a spiritual world, not a physical one. The Root World, called *Adam Kadmon* (The Primeval Man), generated four more worlds, called *Atzilut*, *Beria*, *Yetzira*, and *Assiya*. Those, too, are spiritual worlds, not physical ones.

At the bottom of *Assiya* was a black point, called "the point of This World," which materialized into what you and I know as "the universe." Within our universe there is a galaxy, called the Milky Way, and in that galaxy there is a tiny planet called Earth.

Earth's evolution from fiery lava to cool seas to the upheaval of mountains and the break-up of landmass into the continents continued for many millions of years. It is the physical parallel of the spiritual Root Phase. When Earth cooled, vegetative life began, which reigned the globe for several million years.

On Course

When we talk about moving from inanimate to vegetative, to animate, and to human, we automatically think of Darwin, or of the explanation of creation that suits our belief system. But you should know that according to Kabbalah, the only reason for the appearance of the next step of creation—or of anything else, for that matter—is the completion of the previous step. When a phase is completed, the very end of the phase is the incentive for the appearance of the next stage in line.

Life on Earth continued to evolve until, at some point, the first animals appeared.

The last animal to evolve was, you guessed it, man. Humans first appeared several tens of thousands of years ago. They first lived like animals, finding whatever food was available.

Gradually, humans evolved and became the first animal to ask about the origin of its own existence. The name of the first person to ask where he came from was Adam. Yes, *that* Adam. This is why Adam is considered by Kabbalists as the first person to reach spirituality, to discover the source of his own existence—and yours, too.

If you look back at this short history of evolution, you will notice that it always consists of five phases before a major change occurs. Kabbalists describe five phases, five spiritual worlds, and five stages in the physical world: inanimate, vegetative, animate, human, and spiritual.

ADAM

Adam, partner of Eve and temporary resident of the Garden of Eden, marks the beginning of the final phase in evolution: the spiritual phase. In Kabbalah, Adam is considered the Root Phase of human spirituality. This is why he is called *Adam ha Rishon*, The First Man.

Adam was also the first person to write a Kabbalah book, *HaMalaach Raziel* (*The Angel of God's Secret*), a small book that included a few drawings and tables. (It should be noted that even though Kabbalists ascribe this work to Adam, there is no written proof that he is indeed its author.) The name *HaMalaach Raziel* comes from the Hebrew words *Malaach* (angel), *Raz* (secret), and *El* (God). Thus, *HaMalaach Raziel* reveals to us the secrets of the Creator.

Off Course

Kabbalah books are packed with vivid descriptions of anything from two people walking and talking to their donkey driver to flying towers. As a result, we can be easily misled into thinking that there are worlds where these things happen on a physical level. They do not. All the stories in Kabbalah describe one's connection to the Creator, one's level of altruism, and one's efforts to become one. This is why it is so important to study with a teacher who can provide the correct explanations, which bring you "down to Earth."

The Kabbalistic tradition has it that Adam wrote *The Angel of God's Secret* more than 5,769 years ago. Adam used allegories and metaphors to tell us how he sensed that he lived in two worlds, the earthly and the spiritual. He felt the entire Upper Existence, but he could not describe it in a manner we can relate to today. He attained it in his feelings and thus pictured it the best way he could.

If you browse *The Angel of God's Secret*, it is evident that the author is not an uncivilized, uneducated mammoth hunter. Adam was a Kabbalist of a very high degree who discovered the fundamental secrets of creation in his spiritual journey. He studied the Upper World, where our souls roam prior to their descent to Earth when we are born, and where the souls return after death. Adam tells us how these souls will regroup into one soul and build what we call "man," of which we are but fragments. More on how that works in Chapter 8.

ABRAHAM

Abraham came 20 generations after Adam and was the first to conduct organized Kabbalah studies. He saw the wonders of human existence and asked questions of the Creator, and thus discovered the Upper Worlds.

Abraham passed the knowledge and the method he used to acquire the Upper Worlds to the generations following him. In this way, Kabbalah was transferred from teacher to students for many centuries. Each Kabbalist added his unique experience and personality to this body of accumulated knowledge.

Abraham lived in Mesopotamia (today's Iraq) and, as all inhabitants, worshiped the sun, the moon, the stones, and the trees. But one day he began to wonder, "How was the world created?" "Why does everything 'spin' around us?" and "What does life mean?" Indeed, there must be some meaning to life, he thought, a beginning, end, cause and effect. There must be a force that sets everything in motion! Abraham asked himself those questions and, eventually, through the picture of our world, felt and saw the same as Adam did, that he lived in two worlds at once, the spiritual and the material.

And, yes, these are all the very same questions that have begun to bring Kabbalah to the fore in today's society.

Like Kabbalists after him, Abraham wrote about his discoveries. His book, *Sefer Yetzira* (*The Book of Creation*), is the next important text after *HaMalaach Raziel*. Unlike longer Kabbalah books, *Sefer Yetzira* has only several dozen pages.

Abraham's purpose in writing his book was not to teach attainment of the Upper World, but only to mark out a few principal laws that he discovered about the spiritual world, like an outline.

Kabbalists consider it a difficult book to study correctly because it was written for people who lived thousands of years ago. In those days, souls of people were not as coarse as they are today. They could understand the text even though it is written very succinctly. Today we need a much more detailed text to be able to relate to it. This is why Baal HaSulam wrote his commentaries on *The Book of Zohar* and *The Tree of Life*.

When Abraham discovered spirituality, he immediately started disseminating his knowledge. This is why it is written that he would sit at his tent door and invite people in. There, he taught them what he had learned of the spiritual. Eventually, these students that Abraham would invite into his tent became the first study group in the history of Kabbalah.

MOSES

The name *Moshe* (Moses) comes from the Hebrew word *Moshech* (pulling), as in pulling out of this world. Moses was different than other Kabbalists in that alongside his revelations, he was ordered to publicize them in writing and establish learning centers.

Moses had 70 disciples, and Yehoshua Ben Nun (Joshua, the son of Nun) was the one who succeeded him. Moses did more than research the Upper World. He dealt with the practical realization of his spiritual attainment in our world, such as the exodus from Egypt. With the wisdom he acquired and the Upper

Forces he received from Above, he brought the people of Israel out of exile.

His next task was to write a book with which any person could "conquer" the Upper World. With this book, they could exit Egypt in the spirit and stop worshiping idols, the sun, and other false gods. It would grant them entrance to the *spiritual* Israel—*Atzilut*, a world of eternity and wholeness.

Moses created a method in his book, *The Torah* (Pentateuch), from the word *Ohr* (Light). It contains instructions on how to use the Light as a means to advance in the spiritual world. All people can uncover the entire picture of creation; they can reach the desired outcome and achieve the final goal if they only read and understand the instructions correctly. Moses' method from *The Torah*, adapted to today's souls, allows anyone to attain Moses' degree of spirituality.

RASHBI
(RABBI SHIMON BAR YOCHAI)

The Book of Zohar (*The Book of Radiance*), the next major work in Kabbalah and perhaps the most famous, was written by Rabbi Shimon Bar Yochai, "the Rashbi," around the year 150 C.E. Rashbi was a disciple of Rabbi Akiva (40 C.E.–135 C.E.), famed first and foremost for his emphases on the rule, "Love thy friend as thyself."

Rabbi Akiva did not, however, live a similar fate. He and several of his disciples were tortured and killed by the Romans, who felt threatened by his teaching of the Kabbalah. They flayed his skin and stripped his bones with an iron scraper (like today's currycomb) used for cleaning their horses.

Before that, a plague killed almost all of Rabbi Akiva's 24,000 students except a handful, among which was Rabbi Shimon Bar-Yochai. Kabbalists saw this plague as a result of their growing egoism, which led them to unfounded hatred. This was the opposite of their teacher's rule, "Love thy friend as thyself."

Following the death of Rabbi Akiva's 24,000 disciples, Rashbi was authorized by Rabbi Akiva and Rabbi Yehuda Ben Baba to teach future generations the Kabbalah as it had been taught to him. It was felt that only those who hadn't fallen into this unfounded hatred survived and they wrote the next great chapter in Kabbalah, *The Book of Zohar*.

Tidbits

Academics and Kabbalists differ on the question of where and when *The Book of Zohar* was written. Kabbalists trace *The Zohar* back to Rabbi Shimon and the academia to Rabbi Moshe de Leon of thirteenth-century Spain. Baal HaSulam clearly states that *The Zohar* was written from the highest possible spiritual degree. According to him, only one as high as Rabbi Shimon could have written it, and not a Kabbalist at the degree of Moshe De Leon, even though he is a respected Kabbalist. Baal HaSulam even said that *The Zohar* was written from such a high degree that it wouldn't surprise him to discover that Moses himself wrote it.

IN THE CAVE

Rashbi and four others were the only ones to survive the plague and the wrath of the Romans, who killed his teacher. Following the capture and imprisonment of Rabbi Akiva, Rashbi escaped with his son, Rabbi Elazar, to a cave.

After 13 years, they had heard that the Romans were no longer searching for them and they emerged from the cave. Once outside the cave, Rashbi gathered 8 more men, and all 10 (Rashbi, his son, and the men) went to a small cave in Meron, a village in Northern Israel. With the help of his son and the other 8, Rabbi Shimon wrote the pinnacle of Kabbalah books, *The Book of Zohar*, only to hide it soon after it was written.

Rashbi did not write *The Zohar* himself; he dictated the book to Rabbi *Aba*, who phrased it in such a way that only those who are worthy of understanding would be able to do so. After

☺✎ **Tidbits**

The Zohar disappeared for hundreds of years until it was discovered by Arabs, who used its pages as paper to prepare fish for the market. It was later discovered by a hungry Kabbalist.

its writing, when Rabbi Shimon and his pupils saw that their generation wasn't ready for its content, they hid it until the time was ripe and the people were ready. Many prominent Kabbalists say that this time is our time, and indeed *The Zohar* is more in demand today than ever before.

EARLY REAPPEARANCE

The book was discovered earlier, however, purely by accident. It fell into the hands of Kabbalist, Rabbi Moshe De Leon, who kept it and studied it in secret. When he died, his wife sold the book because she had to make ends meet once her husband died, and he probably didn't tell her about its importance. This is why the writing of *The Zohar* is often ascribed to Moshe De Leon, even though Moshe De Leon himself ascribed it to Rashbi.

The Zohar states that it is written for a time when *chutzpah* (impudence) mounts and the face of the generation is as the face of a dog. When prominent Kabbalists such as the Vilna Gaon, Baal HaSulam, and others looked into the future, they declared the present generation as the one that *The Zohar* referred to. Clearly, they didn't mean it as a compliment.

RABBI ISAAC LURIA (THE ARI)

This stage in the development of Kabbalah is extremely important to the Kabbalah of our generation. This is the period of "the Ari," Rabbi Isaac Luria. The Ari proclaimed the start of a period of open mass study of Kabbalah.

Until the arrival of the Ari, the predominant study method was that of the Ramak (Rabbi Moshe Cordovero) of Safed. It was a method where a Kabbalist simply experienced the Upper World, almost intuitively.

When the Ari came to Safed, however, it was clear that times had changed. It was the middle of the 1500s, and the world was moving toward the age of science and industry. The Ari realized that Kabbalah study required a new and more systematic method to meet the terms of a new and more scientific era. Not all agreed so enthusiastically, but the Ramak himself, by then the predominant Kabbalist of his time, abandoned his own method and sat down to learn the new way from the new teacher, the Ari. Many brows were raised at this step, but the 36-year-old Ari knew what the generation needed, and the Ramak acknowledged it.

A METHOD THAT SUITS ITS TIME

Rabbi Isaac Luria was born in Jerusalem in 1534. A child when his father died, his mother took him to Egypt, where he grew up in his uncle's home. During his life in Egypt, he made his living in commerce but devoted most of his time to studying Kabbalah. Legend has it that he spent 7 years in isolation on the island of Roda, on the Nile, where he studied *The Zohar*, books by the first Kabbalists, and writings of the Ramak.

The Ari arrived in Safed, Israel, in 1570. Despite his youth, he immediately started teaching Kabbalah. For a year and a half, his disciple, Rav Chaim Vital, committed to paper the answers to many of the questions that arose during his studies. In fact, the Ari didn't write anything himself. "The writings of the Ari" are in fact, the notes that Chaim Vital took while studying with his master.

The Ari's important works include *The Tree of Life*, *Mavo She'arim* (*Entrance to the Gates*), *Sha'ar HaKavanot* (*The Gateway of Intentions*), and *Sha'ar HaGilgulim* (*The Gateway of Reincarnation*). The unique part of the Ari's method is its systematic order, which was suitable for the approaching era of the scientific and industrial revolution.

Today, his method, called "Lurianic Kabbalah," is the leading study method of Kabbalah, since it is adapted to the souls of today's humanity. The Ari died of a sudden illness in 1572, still a young man.

The writings of Kabbalah shed a unique light on history and can be said to comprise a history of the Light of the Creator. During most of this time, however, Kabbalah was hidden, studied in the dark, away from the public eye. It was a private affair and, for the most part, even secretive.

With the prophecies of *The Zohar* and the work of the Ari, Kabbalah was meant to shed its light on all. The journey of how Kabbalah sheds its light publicly continues with the work of Rabbi Yehuda Ashlag, who, as the next chapter shows, opened the study of Kabbalah to more people than ever.

IN A NUTSHELL

- The Creation according to Kabbalah consists of five phases.
- Adam was the first Kabbalist and is said to have authored the book *The Angel of God's Secret*.
- Abraham started the first "Kabbalah group" through his teaching and wrote *The Book of Creation*.
- Moses is the force that pulls us out of egoism and into spirituality. He wrote the Torah (Pentateuch).
- *The Book of Zohar*, the seminal book in Kabbalah, predicted its own reemergence at the end of time. Kabbalists say that the end of time is our time.
- The Ari created the scientific method of teaching Kabbalah that is the predominant teaching method today. The book he is most famed for is *The Tree of Life*.

6

BAAL HASULAM

JUST THE GIST
- The goal of Kabbalah
- The benefit in Kabbalah books
- Baal HaSulam and his commentaries on *The Zohar* and the writings of the Ari
- Baal HaSulam's mission
- The urgency in revealing Kabbalah

Kabbalah wasn't always as popular as it is today. When it first started, it was in demand by only a few, who searched for the meaning of their lives. These first Kabbalists continued to develop it through the generations, adapted it to the changing times and made it more scientific, as our generation demands. This chapter introduces the way Kabbalistic texts work and how they have developed over the centuries to make their wisdom more available and accessible to everyone.

In particular, this chapter discusses the work of the most "universal" of all Kabbalists: Rav Yehuda Ashlag. Rav Ashlag clearly stated that Kabbalah study is open for all, that Kabbalah can be disclosed, distributed, and taught to everyone, without any consideration of age, race, sex, or religion.

THE GOAL OF KABBALAH

The goal of Kabbalah is to create a method for individuals to become spiritually fulfilled. As you know by now, *Kabbalah* means "reception." The purpose of life in this world is for a person to achieve the highest level of spirituality.

According to Kabbalah, souls repeatedly come back to this world in people until their goal is reached. The spiritual goal is different from creative and intellectual aspirations. As described in Chapter 4, the quest for spirituality is the final stage of human development. Kabbalah guides and offers a path to spiritual fulfillment.

WHAT KABBALAH BOOKS DO FOR YOU, AND WHAT THEY DON'T

Kabbalist writers describe their experiences and offer recommendations so others can follow in their path. Kabbalah books are accounts of their journeys into the Upper World.

Off Course

The use of mundane words in Kabbalah, like drinking, sitting, mating, and animal names, leads to false conceptions and erroneous conclusions because it makes us think of physical objects as having any spiritual merit. And they don't. They only symbolize spiritual states. Hence, Kabbalah forbids imagining a connection between the names used in our world and their spiritual roots. This is considered the grossest error in Kabbalah.

Kabbalah books are also filled with drawings that illustrate spiritual concepts and events. It is important to remember that the shapes in the drawings are not real objects, but images used to explain *spiritual* states concerning your relationship with the Creator.

But Kabbalah books don't show you the whole picture. To really know what the spiritual worlds look and feel like, you have to experience them for yourself. Kabbalists think of themselves as tour guides whose job is to get you to a place and let you admire it for yourself. This is why, in texts that were written to teach, the descriptions you'll find are partial, displaying only what you need to know to get to spirituality yourself. Such "didactic" texts are Rashbi's *The Book of Zohar*, the Ari's *The Tree of Life*, and Yehuda Ashlag's *The Study of the Ten Sefirot*.

ROOTS—FROM TOP TO BOTTOM

Kabbalah explains that the roots of our world are spiritual roots, coming down from Above, not from below. Roots come from the source, which is Above this world. Picture roots growing in from the outside of a bubble. Because you are in the bubble, the area of creation, the roots come down to you. They can be thought of as colorful party streamers hanging from above.

The main goal of this wisdom is for the Creator to reveal his Godliness to his creatures (that's us). Each root has its own branch in this world, and everything in this world is a branch of some root in spirituality. In this way, Kabbalists "use" this world to communicate with the Creator and to learn His ways, so that they can become like Him.

To avoid "miscommunication" with the Creator, you need to know which branch relates to which root. The arrival of the Ari and, to a greater extent, that of Rav Ashlag, marked a shift toward a new and clearer terminology in Kabbalah. Kabbalists describe their internal experiences and understandings using metaphors and a language suitable for the souls of their time. Over time, their texts become unclear because people's souls develop and require new explanations. This requires of succeeding Kabbalists to write interpretations to make the spiritual journey clearer and more accessible for us. This is why Rav Ashlag wrote a commentary on *The Tree of Life*, published in his major work *The Study of the Ten Sefirot*.

Rav Ashlag's commentary on *The Tree of Life* details the stages, events, and forms of life's creation, originally described by the Ari. Ashlag did a similar thing with Rashbi's *The Book of Zohar*: he took Rashbi's text and clarified it in a commentary he called *HaSulam* (The Ladder). This is why Rabbi Yehuda Ashlag is also known as Baal HaSulam (Owner of the Ladder).

THE GREAT COMMENTATOR

Born in 1884 in Warsaw, Poland, Baal HaSulam studied Kabbalah with the Rabbi Yehoshua of Porsov, and absorbed written and oral law. He became a judge and teacher in Warsaw as early as the age of 19. In 1921, he immigrated to Israel (then called Palestine) with his family (including his first-born son, Baruch, who later succeeded him) and became the rabbi of *Givat Shaul* in Jerusalem. While writing many other important works, such as *The Study of the Ten Sefirot*, he also began *The Sulam Commentary on The Zohar* in 1943. He finished just 10 years later, in 1953. He died the following year and is buried in Jerusalem.

Baal HaSulam is the only one who succeeded in composing complete (and updated) commentaries of *The Zohar* and the writings of the Ari since they were first written. His books allow Kabbalists to study ancient texts in modern language and are indispensable tools for those who aspire to achieve spirituality.

In his article "Time to Act," Baal HaSulam explains that before the printing press, when scribes were in vogue, no one would bother bending their back to copy a book with wild claims; it wouldn't be worth the time, expense, and candle wax. As bookmaking advanced, theories and connections to Kabbalah were enhanced by authors, which were easily published.

With many people trying to define it, an atmosphere of frivolity developed around Kabbalah. Therefore, Ashlag's goal in his writing was to reveal what he could of its true essence.

In his "Introduction to The Book of Zohar," Ashlag says that he must write Kabbalah books because every generation has its own needs, and therefore its own books. Our generation, too, requires books that we can all understand. Since the books of the Ari were written hundreds of years ago, and *The Book of Zohar* was written almost 2,000 years ago, he has taken it on himself to interpret them for us. This way, we can come to know

Off Course

These days, Kabbalah has attained a kind of popularity and notoriety often ascribed to the latest fads. If that is the reason for your study, you will likely be disappointed for two reasons. It does not provide easy answers, and to approach it as the latest fad is to completely misunderstand what it's about. On the other hand, if you study it with an honest desire to come in touch with your spiritual nature, you're likely to be thoroughly satisfied by this study. However, even if you're looking for easy answers and something resonates here, that's all for the good as well.

what these ancient Kabbalists knew, and experience the spiritual worlds for ourselves.

CALL OF THE HOUR

But the spreading of Kabbalah is happening today not only as a result of the appearance of incorrect and inaccurate books. Ashlag explains, in his "Introduction to The Book of Zohar" and in many of his essays, that the spreading of Kabbalah is a must today. He explains that now is the time that Prophet Jeremiah referred to when he said, "for they shall all know Me, from the least of them unto the greatest of them."

We can take our time and let it happen naturally, but Ashlag says that such a decision will cost us heavily, because we would be compelled to evolve into spirituality by nature itself. He says that the other option is to study what nature wants of us and do it.

This, according to Ashlag, will not only prevent the suffering he was talking about, but will show us how to receive the pleasures that the Creator wants to give us. Ancient Kabbalists called these two choices "in due time" or "accelerating time."

Today, according to Ashlag, it is no longer a mere "good idea" to share the knowledge; it is the call of the hour. Hence, without further ado let's dive into the heart of the wisdom and its concepts.

IN A NUTSHELL

- Kabbalah provides a method for attaining spiritual fulfillment.
- Rav Yehuda Ashlag is credited with making older, difficult-to-read Kabbalah texts easier to interpret.
- Kabbalah study has evolved into a systematic and scientific method of study.
- The wisdom of Kabbalah disappears and reappears when the time for its insights is ripe, and now the time is ripe.

II

Before
there
Was Time

Curious about why we were created?

Questions about the meaning of life and why we are here have been asked since the beginning of time, so join the rest of the world in your queries. But the answers may be more easily understood than you thought.

Kabbalists seek to understand the questions of the purpose of life, and all it takes to begin your own understanding is to ask. In this section, you'll learn some pure Kabbalah knowledge and find some of the answers to those age-old mysteries.

7
Down and Up the Ladder

JUST THE GIST

- A ladder was made as we came down; now we can use it to climb back up
- 125 spiritual degrees
- *Reshimot*—your spiritual databank—and what you can do with them.
- Free choice and the choice of your friends

In his "Introduction to The Book of Zohar," Baal HaSulam depicts three states that souls experience. The first state is the beginning of creation, which contains everything that will later evolve in the soul, like a seed contains the plant that will grow. The second state is the birth of the soul, somewhat like the seed's stages of growth. The third state is when the soul realizes its potential to the fullest, reaches the level of the Creator, and bonds with Him. In the third state, the soul returns to the first state, but this time it is a conscious and mature act.

Another way to think of these stages is like a baby's growth: in the first stage the child is at its mother's height because she's holding it next to her chest. In stage two, the child stands and begins to grow from below. In the third and last stage, the child has become fully grown, once more reaching the mother's level, but this time as a conscious and mature adult.

THE FIVE-RUNG LADDER

The cycle of spiritual reality is like a ladder. This ladder is probably not available at your local hardware store, but you could ask. The Spiritual Light is at the top of the ladder. It is the starting point, the zero, or Root point, in Kabbalistic language. The starting point is Phase Zero, which we introduced in Chapter 5, but here we are referring to it as the beginning of the circle, hence the different name. Kabbalists often use different names to the same spiritual states, to emphasize a different function of the same spiritual entity or degree.

The Light came down in four steps: 1, 2, 3, 4. Because the cycle starts at the root or zero, Kabbalah's ladder has five stages and four steps. A barrier at the end of Phase 4 stops the spiritual Light, except for a fraction of Light, which evolves into our universe.

Note the similarity to the five levels of human desire presented in Chapter 4. Kabbalah is a system in which cycles in one aspect of existence match cycles in another. The five levels of desire in our world correspond to the five cycles in the spiritual reality of the Upper Worlds. As you will see throughout this chapter, the number 5 reappears in Kabbalah in different ways, describing different aspects of an overall Kabbalistic journey to spiritual attainment.

The fraction of Light that went through the barrier continued to evolve, and Earth was formed. The planet cooled and vegetative life appeared, then animals, humans, and finally humans who are reaching the last degree of evolution—the desire for spirituality. So the Creator came "down" the ladder to Earth, and Kabbalah helps us follow the same path "up" the ladder to the Creator, which the Creator took to get "down" to us.

FIVE PHASES OR FIVE SEFIROT

Because the Creator started out by giving, this is the foundation for the relationship with the Creator, marked by five phases of spiritual development. The starting point for you and I involves receiving. The Creator gives, and we receive.

So Phase Zero is the Creator, the desire to give, and happily receiving is Phase 1 in the cycle of spirituality. But the Creator gave humans more than a mere desire to enjoy. He gave us the desire to become like Him because what could be better than being like Him? Because being like the Creator is even better than mere receiving, Phase 2 is wanting to give, and in this case, it means wanting to give back to the Creator.

In Phase 3, we (the created beings) understand that the only way to give to the Creator is to do what He wants because there is nothing else we can give Him. Because He wants us to receive, that's what we do in Phase 3. But note the difference: this isn't like the receiving in Phase 1. Here, in Phase 3 we receive because He wants to give, not because we wish to receive. Our *intention* has changed from receiving for ourselves to receiving for the Creator. This, in Kabbalah, is considered giving.

Phase 3 could have been the end of the process if it hadn't been for this tiny issue called "the third stage." We previously said that our goal is not merely to be attached to the Creator, but to become like Him. This can only happen when we have His Thoughts, when we know and actually participate in the Thought of Creation. Therefore, Phase 4 introduces a new thrill: the desire to understand the actual Thought of Creation. Here you want to understand what the giving is for, what makes it

Kabbalearn

The whole business with the *Sefirot* may sound confusing, but it is less so if we remember that they stand for desires. *Keter* is the Creator's desire to give Light (pleasure); *Hochma* is our reception of the pleasure; *Bina* stands for our desire to give back to the Creator; *ZA* is our desire to receive in order to give to the Creator; and *Malchut* is our pure desire to receive, the actual root of the creatures—us.

pleasurable, why giving creates everything, and what wisdom it provides.

The four phases and their root each have a second name. Phase Zero is also called *Keter*, Phase 1—*Hochma*, Phase 2—*Bina*, Phase 3—*Tifferet* or *Zeir Anpin* (ZA), and Phase 4—*Malchut*. These additional names are called *Sefirot* (Sapphires), because they shine like sapphires.

THE SCREEN (AND THE UNLIKELY EXAMPLE)

The Creator did not instill in us the wish to be like Him, however. In Phase 4, you decide that you will receive only if you understand *why* the Creator wants to give—until you understand what's in it for Him.

For example, imagine that you offer to take your children to the mall to buy them whatever they want. Unlikely, granted. Now imagine that they say to you, "Why are you suggesting that? What does that do for you? If we don't understand why you are giving, we're not interested in the gifts." Far more unlikely. This conditioning of not receiving for yourself is called *Tzimtzum* (restriction). It is the first thing we do to become non-egoistic, and the mechanism that enables the *Tzimtzum* is called a *Masach* (screen).

Once we have acquired a *Masach* we can begin to calculate if and how much we can receive while focusing on our parents' pleasure instead of our own. When we acquire this ability, it is considered that we have a complete *Partzuf* (face).

5 × 5 × 5

The five phases of spiritual development correspond to five spiritual worlds, and each spiritual world contains five *Partzufim* (faces). To continue the ladder metaphor, the worlds begin at the top of the ladder, closest to the Creator, and continue on down. The worlds, from to bottom, are *Adam Kadmon*, *Atzilut*, *Beria*, *Yetzira*, and *Assiya*. The world closest to the Light and the Creator, *Adam Kadmon*, is also the most spiritual. The other worlds move downward, becoming more "material" and less "spiritual" as they descend.

> **On Course**
>
> It is important to try to understand the five worlds because the effort itself brings you closer to them, just as we feel naturally close to a person who wants to be like us. Besides, even if you don't understand them as you study, you will understand them when you climb the spiritual ladder yourself because you will discover that these worlds already exist within you. They are part of your spiritual makeup, just as they are part of creation's makeup.

Our task is to attain the highest degree in our advancement toward the Creator. There are 125 degrees in the spiritual ladder that move you up through these five worlds. Why the number 125? Because there are 5 worlds, and 5 *Partzufim* in each world, and 5 *Sefirot* (*Keter–Malchut*) in each *Partzuf*. Therefore, 5×5×5 equals 125. (You may have noticed that Kabbalists have a thing with numbers.)

Note that our world does not count as a *spiritual degree*. The degrees begin Above our world and move up. *Assiya* is the closest spiritual world to our own and the starting point of spiritual attainment.

> **Kabbalearn**
>
> Two elements make up a spiritual degree: a *desire* for something and the *intention* to use it for the Creator.

The advancement from one degree to the next happens only when a person has experienced the full measure of desire in the present degree, with the pure intention to give to the Creator. A higher degree is characterized by a greater desire for pleasure and a stronger intention to give that pleasure to the Creator.

The smallest element in spirituality is called *Sefira* because it shines like a sapphire. We already said that there are five basic *Sefirot*: *Keter, Hochma, Bina, Zeir Anpin,* and *Malchut.* However, *Zeir Anpin* (ZA) is made of six internal *Sefirot*: *Hesed, Gevura, Tifferet, Netzah, Hod,* and *Yesod.* So whether we talk about the five *Sefirot—Keter, Hochma, Bina,* ZA, and *Malchut—*or about the 10 *Sefirot—Keter, Hochma, Bina, Hesed, Gevura, Tifferet, Netzah, Hod, Yesod,* and *Malchut—*it refers to the same basic structure of 10 *Sefirot.*

Each five *Sefirot* make up one *Partzuf* (face), and five *Partzufim* make up one *Olam* (world). Interestingly, the word *Olam* comes from the Hebrew word *Ha'alama,* which means "concealment." The higher the *Olam,* the less there is *Ha'alama* (of the Creator). So when you get to the Higher Worlds, too, you'll know where you are by seeing what's around you and comparing it with the "tour guide"—the Kabbalah books.

One of the mechanisms of this progression and development is the concept of *Tzimtzum* (restriction), which we mentioned earlier. It works like this: if you have a desire for object A, but a much stronger desire for object B, then your desire for object A gets *Tzimtzumed* (restricted). For example, say you're very tired and want to go to sleep. You tuck yourself in and cuddle under the warm blanket. Suddenly, someone knocks on your door and shouts that there is a fire and that you'd better run for your life. Naturally, your desire to save yourself is stronger than your desire to sleep. At that moment the fatigue vanishes as if it never existed. In truth, it does exist, and you will feel it again when the danger has passed, but the desire to live restricts it and covers it completely.

Turning back to our topic, to move from degree *x* to degree *x+1*, we need to want degree *x+1* more than our present *x* degree.

In *The Study of the Ten Sefirot*, Baal HaSulam says that even though *Malchut*, the *Sefira* that represents the future us, wanted to receive the Creator's Light very much, she couldn't. *Malchut* didn't know how to receive the Light with the intention to give (remember the mall example from earlier in this chapter). Without the intention to give, she would become different from the Creator and, therefore, separated from Him. Because she did not want to become separated from the Creator, she restricted her desire to receive so she could stay close to the Creator.

This is why the first thing you must learn when entering the spiritual world is how to restrict your egoistic desires. If you can't do that, the doors to spirituality remain closed, which brings us to the Barrier.

THE FIFTH LEVEL AND THE BARRIER

The sole purpose of everything that happens in our world is to take you across the barrier between our world and the spiritual world. Once you cross it, you can start advancing in spirituality.

Where did this barrier come from? You may recall that contact with the Creator can exist only if you, like Him, have the intention to give. Because He created you without the intention to give, you are separated from Him. This separation is called a barrier because it bars you from direct contact with Him. The good news is that you can cross the barrier and meet the Creator "face to face" simply by wanting the intention to give.

Kabbalah has many divisions. One division is into *Sefirot*, another is into worlds, and another is into levels of vitality.

So spiritual as well as corporal life is divided into five levels of vitality:

1. Still (inanimate)
2. Vegetative
3. Animate (alive)
4. Speaking (human)
5. Spiritual (point in the heart)

Every being has all five levels, but the predominant level determines its category. Animals, for example, have some characteristics that are typically human, such as the ability to plan for the future, but this is not their predominant trait. Humans have animalistic characteristics, too, but we are still fundamentally different from animals.

What makes people human in the spiritual sense is their ability to experience a uniquely human state: the desire to be spiritual (like the Creator), the point in the heart. This is the highest state, where you can cross the barrier into the spiritual realm.

Kabbalearn

The voluntary and conscious evolution at the human level is what we call "free choice." Free choice makes us similar to the Creator because we choose to be like Him.

Achieving this stage involves different factors than the first four levels of vitality, which are based on biological factors. Levels 1-4 evolve through pressures from nature that push evolution along unconsciously. But evolution to the fifth level is voluntary and conscious, made out of one's own *free choice*. A desire for it is the first step to crossing the barrier. It's the desire mentioned in the beginning of this book, the desire to ask what life is about, the desire upon which Kabbalah itself is based.

THE START OF THE CLIMB

At the bottom rung on the spiritual ladder, where you and I start, we are disconnected from the Creator. Here, the task is to refurbish our desire for spirituality and make it a working vehicle to drive us up the spiritual ladder once more.

All souls started out at being one with the Creator. In a sense, then, you and I have been developing and refurbishing ourselves for many thousands of years. In the framework of Kabbalah, the last 6,000 years have been the culmination of this process. Now the process is nearing its end, a time when all of humanity is becoming spiritual. So let's look at the process and see how Kabbalah shows a way to go about this spiritual process.

TOWARDS A COMMON SOUL

Kabbalah provides a method for spiritual correction and specifies a 6,000-phase route, referred to in the literature as "6,000 years." After their complete correction, all souls reunite into one common soul and start working as a unified system. The construction of this common soul binds the individual souls together so that each of them feels what all the others feel. This is the achievement of absolute attainment, called the "End of Correction."

The only thing necessary to embark on this spiritual journey is the desire to do so. No spiritual progress can possibly occur in you if you do not want it beforehand. At the spiritual degree, evolution should be conscious and voluntary.

Questions such as "Why am I suffering?" "Where does pain come from and what does it want of me?" "Is there a purpose to suffering?" and "Is it all worthwhile?" are useful if the predicaments give you the sense to ask for directions on how to evolve. They are even more useful if you can use them to increase your desire for spirituality. When you begin to ask yourself these questions, it is a sure sign that you've begun your way up the spiritual ladder.

UP THE LADDER

The desire to be spiritual is the first step up the ladder. You start by wanting to fulfill this desire, and you will obtain it by simply asking (in your heart). Asking to be more spiritual is called "raising MAN" (Aramaic: *Mayin Nukvin*—Female Water). Raising MAN is also called a prayer. MAN, or desire to be more spiritual, comes from two sources: One is your own spiritual structure, *Reshimot*. These are the soul's unconscious recollections of its past states. The second is the environment (friends, books, films, and all other media), which enhances and speeds up the MAN that the *Reshimot* evoke.

> **⚠ Off Course**
>
> The environment can speed you up, but it can also slow you down. If you surround yourself with people, books, and media that do not appreciate spirituality, (that is, altruism), you, too, will not want it. Once you've placed yourself in a certain society, you cannot choose your thoughts; you subconsciously absorb them from the environment. The free choice we *do* have, however, is in the environment itself. Choosing the right environment will lead to or from spirituality, and determine our speed.

BACK TO THE FUTURE

If you remember at the beginning of the chapter, we stated that the Root was the beginning, at the top of the ladder. Although it may seem like a contradiction, it's important to remember it because it means that you and I contain the seeds of the Root within us—the seeds of the Creator, if you will.

So the Root is both the beginning of the cycle of spirituality and our ultimate goal. Having "fallen," you and I seek to regain the top, or correct ourselves. That requires climbing the spiritual ladder, from the earthly world back up to the Root. To understand how to return to your Root, you need to know your root and how you came down from there (the *Reshimot*).

How else could you know where to return if you hadn't already been there in some way? The emergence of new desires, new *Reshimot*, indicates that you are making progress, how fast you are progressing, and if you're on the best and fastest route. In the end, we will all reach the end of correction, but a correct use of the *Reshimot* can save us much trouble, time, and effort.

You move up the ladder each time you increase your desire to be spiritual. As you become more spiritual, you build on the last degree of spirituality to achieve the next. Every time you increase your need, your future spiritual degree responds by elevating you to

Off Course

Kabbalah explains that the spiritual path is predetermined, but this does not mean that you do not have free will and choices. You will be on the same path, but you can progress faster or slower, pleasantly or painfully, *depending on your participation.*

it. The cycle repeats itself and moves you to become more like the Creator.

Once you have examined all your egoistic desires on the egoistic level, called "this world," a new desire appears. This new desire is special. It is your first desire with a non-egoistic intention. This event in a Kabbalist's life, though it is a natural evolution of the surfacing of the desires (*Reshimot*), is so radical that it is known as "The Crossing of the Barrier," or "the admittance to the spiritual world."

At any state your soul is in, the *Reshimo* (singular for *Reshimot*) is predetermined. If you have an urge to realize the *Reshimo*, this urge stems from within. But if you use the environment to strengthen your desire and accelerate the unfolding of the *Reshimo*, that would not only shorten the unfolding period, but also elevate the experience to the spiritual level and make it adventurous and exciting.

WHAT GOES AROUND
COMES AROUND

Life shows us that we cannot survive without a sufficient number of people around, to serve and help provide for our needs. Humans are social beings, and society is like a machine where each individual in like a wheel, linked to other wheels. A single wheel cannot move by itself. However, it joins the motion of all the other wheels and helps the machine perform its purpose.

On Course

In Kabbalah, the collective group and the individual are treated as one and the same. What is good for the whole is good for the individual, and vice versa. Therefore, a negative society harms the individual, and a positive society benefits the individual.

If the wheel breaks, the problem is not the wheel's problem, but the problem of the whole machine because the broken wheel stops the machine from running. It turns out that we are not evaluated for who or what we are, but for the kind of service we do for society. A "bad" person is only as bad as he or she harms the public, not because he or she didn't perform up to the level of some abstract value of good.

Good and bad attributes and deeds are good or bad according to whether they benefit the public. If a part of the group does not contribute its share, those individuals not only harm the collective, but they, too, are harmed. This is why a negative society harms the individual.

Likewise, a good society benefits the individual. Individuals are part of the whole, and the whole is not worth more than the sum of its individuals. In Kabbalah, the collective and the individual are one and the same.

One of the key ideas to understand about Kabbalah is that people will come to see that their own benefit and the benefit of the collective are the same. As people realize that, the world will be much closer to its full correction.

Kabbalah explains that our experiences are personal, but they are described in general terms that apply to everyone. For example, we all agree that blood is red when we look at it, but we each experience it very differently. Some people faint at the sight of blood, some say "Cool!", and some say "Ugh!"

IN A NUTSHELL

- In the spiritual cycle, our souls started at being like the Creator. Then they climbed down the ladder, and now we must travel up it and become like Him again.
- Crossing the barrier into the spiritual realm is done only through a conscious desire to be like the Creator.
- Kabbalah allots 6,000 years for all souls to achieve correction, which can be experienced as a joyous and exciting journey or as an ordeal.
- If we want to reach spirituality, we have to choose a spiritually supportive environment made up of friends, books, and all kinds of media.
- Everything else is determined by the *Reshimot*, except for our choice of environment.

8

SETTING THE STAGE FOR MAN

JUST THE GIST

- The five worlds and the world without end
- The Creator's wish in creating us
- Adam, Eve, and their relationship with the Creator
- Many people, one soul, one correction

This chapter is the heart of the book, the core of Kabbalah. Here, we focus more on the individual in the process and less on degrees, worlds, and *Partzufim*. When you learn it, you will grasp the essence of the Kabbalistic journey toward spirituality, and how Kabbalah provides a way for humanity to correct itself for the good of all.

FIVE WORLDS, AND NONE REAL

As we've mentioned in Chapter 7, there are five spiritual worlds: *Adam Kadmon, Atzilut, Beria, Yetzira,* and *Assiya.* The only thing that is real is the world of *Ein Sof* (No End). We also explained that the word *Olam* (World) comes from word *Ha'alama* (concealment). Therefore, the worlds are incomplete appearances of the Creator. The only place where He is completely revealed is therefore the world of *Ein Sof*, where there are no limitations, hence the name *Ein Sof*, no end to our perception of the Creator.

> Spiritual Sparks
>
> All the worlds, Upper and lower, are contained within.
>
> — Rav Yehuda Ashlag,
> "Introduction to the Preface to the Wisdom of Kabbalah"

The Upper Worlds affect objects in the worlds below, as all the worlds are essentially the same reality—that of *Ein Sof*. For example, if you thought about doing something, and knew for certain that that thought would come true, then your plan would be experienced as existing in you, even before the thought has actually been carried out. Our body knows this process very well; this is why the stomach produces digestive juices before the food actually gets there. In that sense, the thought of eating is a higher world, which creates the lower world where the eating occurs. But in both worlds the event (substance) is the same—eating. Because our thought is not limited, you could say that it is in the world of *Ein Sof*, and our body is in one of the lower worlds.

Keep in mind that although Kabbalah speaks only about the spiritual worlds, it uses physical examples, such as eating, to explain them. Although the examples are used to understand *how* things work in spirituality, don't be misled into thinking that there is physical eating (as in the last example) in spirituality.

AT THE TOP OF THE LADDER

We previously defined Kabbalah as a sequence of causes and consequences that hang down from root to branch, whose purpose is the revelation of the Creator to the creatures. But how do Kabbalists know that? As they reach the top of the spiritual ladder, they discover two things: that creation is made of pure, unadulterated desire to receive pleasure, and that the Creator is made of pure, unadulterated desire to give it to creation.

Off Course
Discussing what the Creator wants is dangerous because it can lead us to thinking about the Creator instead of our own correction, which is what is needed if we want to become like Him. What Kabbalists discover once they reach the Creator's level isn't written anywhere, but we, too, can get there and find out for ourselves.

This brings up another question: If the Creator's only wish is to give, where did creation's pure desire to receive come from? Kabbalists explain that the Creator had to create us; otherwise, He wouldn't have anyone to give to. This is the beginning of the root and branch sequence.

EQUAL BUT OPPOSITE

Kabbalists called the desire "to do good to the creatures" (us), the Thought of Creation. If we keep this in mind, the whole wisdom of Kabbalah will be easy to learn.

If I want to give, like the Creator, there is nothing that can limit me, because you can't "lock" a desire in a certain place or time. Of course, we, people, are also unlimited—we want only to receive, and that desire is just as unlimited as the desire to give. In that sense, we are equal to but opposite from the Creator: our orientation is toward receiving, and His is toward giving.

Another element that becomes clearer when we understand the Thought of Creation is why it takes giving to create. When you want to give, you're looking outwardly, to see where you can do good. But when you want to receive, you are concentrated on yourself, and want only to take from what already exists. Now let's look at the stages of creation.

A SHORT STORY OF CREATION

The story of creation started with a root (His desire to do good to His creations), and expanded in four more phases. This is the origin of the Tree of Life, its first root, if you will. In Phase 4 creation restricted itself, performed a *Tzimtzum*, and rejected all the Light (pleasure) that the Creator wanted to give. Such an act seems to contradict the very Thought of Creation, but it is a necessary step in determining creation as a separate and independent entity from the Creator.

The power by which creation stops receiving the Light is a very special kind of shame, the root of all disgraces, called "the bread of shame." Kabbalists explain that shame is the most powerful force that drives us.

Now hold tight, because we're about to plunge deep into the heart of man: the bread of shame is the mother of all shames. It is an experience unlike anything in this world. It is a burning sensation that has only one name fitting for it: Hell. But don't worry, in Kabbalah no bad comes without its compensation and reward immediately following.

The main difference between our (worldly) shame and the (spiritual) bread of shame is that in our world we are ashamed of not meeting society's standards, and in spirituality we are ashamed of not meeting the Creator's standards.

Imagine that you suddenly discovered that the entire universe, from before the Big Bang until the end of all time, is kind, generous, and giving. Sound great? Now imagine that you also discover that there is only one element in it that's selfish and wants to use everyone and everything else. Well, that must be the devil. Now imagine that you discover that this evil devil is you. What would you do?

Of course, no person can bear it. Then, to top it all off, you discover that the evil is not in your body, it's in your soul, in your desires, so even if you committed suicide you'd still be evil, because no gun can put an end to your soul.

Naturally, when you discover something like that, the last thing you want is to remain yourself, and the thing you want most is to be a giver like the Creator. And the minute you want it, you get it.

Now you know that the *Tzimtzum* isn't a restriction imposed on you. It is the result of your own work of studying yourself. It is also a very rewarding and pleasurable event because it is the first time you receive the ability to actually *be* something else. You can choose not only between two options in this world but also between two entirely different kinds of nature. When you choose one, your senses will show you our world; and when you choose the other, your senses will show you the spiritual world. But you will be able to choose between them and even jump back and forth from one to the other whenever you want.

FOR YOUR PLEASURE ONLY

In Chapter 7, we explained that the worlds, from top to bottom, are *Adam Kadmon, Atzilut, Beria, Yetzira,* and *Assiya.* We also said that each world is made of five interior elements called *Partzufim.* Now let's talk about how they're made and how they work.

On Course

Don't let all the names in Kabbalah confuse you; they refer to either bestowal or reception. Creator, Light, Giver, Thought of Creation, Phase Zero, Root, Root Phase, *Bina,* and others describe the desire to bestow. Creature, *Kli,* receivers, Phase One, and *Malchut* are some examples of the desire to receive. There are so many names because of the subtle differences in each. But in the end, they all refer to bestowal or reception.

Once Phase 4, called *Malchut,* experienced the bread of shame, its oppositeness from the Creator, it set up a condition before Him: "If you want me to enjoy, give me the ability to do it for *your* pleasure, not for mine, because I don't enjoy being an egoist." So the Creator gave her a *Masach,* the screen, to resist the entrance of the Light. Then she said to Him: "Thanks, now give me the ability to decide what to receive and what not to receive. I know that I can't receive anything and still be thinking of your pleasure, so let's start with little bits and pieces of Light." He gave her this ability as well.

Malchut began to receive the Light in five primary categories. Just like the visible Light is made of three basic colors—red, green, and blue—Spiritual Light is made of five basic Lights—*Nefesh, Ruach, Neshama, Haya, Yechida. Nefesh* is the smallest Light, and *Yechida* is the greatest.

Once *Malchut* receives the ability to split the Light into five sections, she begins to receive each of them, but only as long as she can do that while thinking of the Creator. Each time she receives a different Light of the five, she builds a special *Partzuf* to receive it. Thus, she completes her ability to sense the Creator at a certain degree by exploring

On Course

Kabbalah ascribes each element in spirituality a gender tag; an element can't be neutral, but it can "switch" between genders. In general, anything that gives is considered male and anything that receives is considered female. Also, each entity contains male and female elements within it, and uses them according to need. So although everything has its basic gender, it can function as its opposite sex when the need arises.

the five Lights as much as she can without thinking of herself. And because there are five such Lights, each spiritual world contains five *Partzufim*.

Now you also understand why each such phase is called *Olam* (world), meaning concealment. This is the level to which *Malchut* can bare to enjoy the Creator's pleasure without thinking of herself. Naturally, the higher the world, the greater is *Malchut's* ability to enjoy the Creator's Light. This is also the great reward that comes with reaching the world of *Ein Sof* (No End)—there are no limitations on reception of the Creator's pleasures.

THE CONSTRUCTION WORKERS

The spiritual worlds have what could be called a teaching mechanism built into them. They can teach you how to direct your desire to give back to the Creator. Although they run on "auto-pilot" meaning they unfold as a necessary cause and effect process, the guiding principle in each of them is "I will not receive unless it's for the Creator." When a person enters the spiritual worlds, this is what the spiritual worlds teach him or her: how to think more of the Creator and less of him or herself.

Kabbalearn

Upper Worlds and lower worlds do not relate to positions or places but to the value of desires. Higher desires are simply more altruistic than lower desires, which are more egoistic.

In that sense, the relationship between the worlds and the creature is like a group of construction workers teaching a rookie what to do. They teach each task by demonstrating it. Bit by bit, creatures (we) can begin to "fix up their desires" and transform their reception from the Creator into an act of giving.

ADAM AND EVE ARE BORN (AND DROPPED)

In Chapter 7 we said that the last phase (and the greatest desire) is to know the Thought of Creation. To understand the Thought of Creation, it was necessary to create a special *Partzuf*, which would exist in a special world, where this *Partzuf* could study the Thought of Creation of its own free choice. This is how the *Partzuf* of *Adam ha Rishon* was formed. Although *Adam ha Rishon* was not born in our physical world, it was quickly brought here (or should we say, dropped here?), and was given the name Adam, after its task, to be *Domeh* (similar) to the Upper One, the Creator.

If you're wondering where Eve is in this picture, she is very much in there. In Kabbalah, Adam and Eve are two parts of the same *Partzuf*. When Kabbalists want to emphasize the reception in this *Partzuf* they refer to it as Eve, and when they want to focus on its giving capabilities they call it Adam.

TRICKED INTO SINNING

Adam was born in the worlds *Beria*, *Yetzira*, and *Assiya*, but was quickly elevated by them to *Atzilut*, where all the desires are corrected and work only to give to the Creator. In the world of *Atzilut*, Adam worked (received) with small desires, ones he was sure he could use altruistically, with the intention of giving to the Creator. He was told he could do anything, as long as he didn't eat from the Tree of Knowledge, which represents the stronger desires, the ones Adam couldn't use with the intention to give to the Creator.

At this point, Adam was considered holy, a saint. But he was unaware of his own uncorrected desires. What Adam didn't know was that he was placed in the Garden of Eden and allowed to work with his small desires only as an example of how he should work with his coarser desires. So when they first appeared, he didn't know how to handle them, and sinned.

When Adam finally decided to try to receive with the intention to give to the Creator, he failed, and wanted to receive for himself. He discovered that he was totally egoistic in those desires, and this (bread of) shame made him cover himself. In Kabbalistic terms, Adam learned that he was naked, without a *Masach* (screen) to cover his bare (egoistic) desires.

But spirituality is a failsafe mechanism. Once a correction is made, you cannot breach it. As a result of Adam's mistake the *Tzimtzum* was reinstalled and all the Light in *Partzuf Adam ha Rishon* left it, leaving Adam and Eve outside of the Garden of Eden. However, they were not totally alone; they had their memories (*Reshimot*) of the corrected state and the *Reshimot* of their egoism. Those two seemingly bad memories are the most valuable tools for any person who wishes to discover the Creator and correct the relationship that existed between Adam and the Creator and discover His full glory.

SIN—THE WAY OUT OF EVIL

In the Kabbalistic version, the story of the original sin has a twist or two that you may not know. Adam was commanded not to eat from the Tree of Knowledge so he would not entangle himself with desires he couldn't handle. But his internal female, Eve, told him that if he did eat, he would be able to give to the Creator even more than if he didn't. She was right, too, because in doing that, he would be using greater desires to receive in order to give to the Creator. But what Eve didn't know was that to give to the Creator with such strong desires, you need to have a very strong *Masach* to handle them. Adam did not have that. You may justly ask, "Why didn't the Creator tell Adam that he couldn't handle such desires, did He want him to fail? What kind of a giving Creator lets his creation suffer?"

To understand why the Creator did that to Adam, we must remember the Thought of Creation, and that this is what Adam really wanted. To teach Adam about his own desires, the Creator had to expose them to him. And how can you expose a desire to someone without letting him or her experience what that desire feels like?

Off Course
This is a good place to remind ourselves that all that the Torah (Five Books of Moses) and Kabbalah write about unfolds in the spiritual worlds, not in our world.

From the perspective of the Creator no harm was done by Adam's sin because from His perspective, this is just another step toward teaching creation how to receive everything that He wants to give. The greatest gift the Creator can give to us is His Thoughts, so that's what He had to show us. Now that we have this memory in our *Reshimot* we can begin to correct ourselves and learn how to receive it.

TINY GOLD COINS

The first step in the correction of Adam's soul was to split it into "digestible" pieces, small bits of desire that weren't so hard to correct. For this reason his soul shattered into no less than 600,000 pieces. It continued to shatter and splinter and today we have as many pieces of his soul as there are people on Earth. Yes, you understand correctly. We're all parts of the same soul. In Part 3 we'll talk about the practical aspects of this fact.

The splitting happened in the following way: when all the desires in *Adam ha Rishon* had a common intention to bestow upon the Creator, they were united as one. When the intention in the desires was reversed into an aim for self-gratification, each desire sensed itself separated from the others, and the single soul became divided. All souls, therefore, are extensions of the general soul of *Adam ha Rishon* (literally translated as "the first man").

Tidbits

The more egoistic we become, the harder it is correct each bit of soul, and the more we have to divide and multiply.

Here is an allegory by Baal HaSulam that explains the splitting principle: A king needed to send a large quantity of gold coins to his son who lived overseas. He had no messengers that he could trust with a big sum, so he split up the gold coins into pennies and sent them by many messengers. Each messenger decided it was not worth stealing such insignificant loot and delivered it. Once the pennies reached their destination they were reunited into the original large sum.

In the same way, many souls over many days can redeem the fragments after the apple incident. All the pieces combine to successfully complete the original task of receiving all the Light in order to give to the Creator. Our job is to correct our individual portions, the roots of our own souls.

IN A NUTSHELL

- There are five worlds—*Adam Kadmon, Atzilut, Beria, Yetzira,* and *Assiya*—but the only real world is *Ein Sof.*
- Our desires are as strong as the Creator's but our intentions are opposite from His.
- Adam and Eve had to be tricked into sinning
- Adam was born in the worlds *Beria, Yetzira,* and *Assiya,* raised to *Atzilut,* then quickly dropped to our world.
- Eve is the female part of *Partzuf Adam ha Rishon.*
- All people are bits of the common soul of *Adam ha Rishon.*

9

Unlocking the Language of Kabbalah

JUST THE GIST
- It's all about the forces
- Understanding the Language of the Branches
- New meanings of old stories
- Demystifying the language of *The Zohar*

To understand Kabbalah texts, you have to understand the language that it's written in. No, you don't have to learn Hebrew, but you do need to understand the way Kabbalistic texts use stories to present ideas. Stories about people and the world become metaphors for concepts and ideas in the Upper Worlds.

The language of Kabbalah describes how forces from the Upper Worlds act on the objects of this world. Stories and the ideas behind them show how the universe is structured. When read in this way, stories about this world—the stories in the Bible, for instance—take on new meanings.

In this chapter, you start to understand how to unlock Kabbalah knowledge. You see that the roots and branches of Kabbalah language bring out more in the stories than generally meets the eye.

LIKE ROOTS AND BRANCHES

As we've explained in Chapters 7 and 8, the worlds are created by a series of causes and effects. Therefore, "roots" refer to the spiritual forces, which create our world and the people in it. They exist in the spiritual worlds beyond this material one, but they influence and operate on our world.

The roots are like many unseen fingers pushing and prodding a piece of clay—our existence—into a certain form. They mold existence by guiding objects. These objects that the spiritual forces, or roots, guide are the "branches." The branches exist in this world. They have material existence. Every object in this world, including you and me, is a branch of some spiritual root.

Kabbalearn

In Kabbalah, every cause is considered a root and every consequence of the cause is considered a branch. The roots are also referred to as "parents" and the branches are considered their "offspring." The key concept in Kabbalah is that what happens in the roots will happen in the branches.

As their names indicate, roots and branches are connected. Like a tree, one of them you see and the other you don't, yet both are connected.

A tree or plant cannot exist without its roots. Things that happen to the roots show up in the plant. If the roots don't receive enough water, the plant droops. If the roots are fertilized, the plant grows fuller.

Kabbalah describes the same mechanism in people. In the universe described by Kabbalah, what happens in the roots shows up in the branches. Just as a plant is affected by the condition of its roots, the forces in the spiritual worlds influence people and objects in this world.

In Chapter 8 we said that the elements in all the worlds are the same. We said that the only difference between them is in the spiritual level of the same elements: the higher worlds contain more altruistic elements and events. So clearly, the objects of each world relate to the objects Above or below it. Forces from one appear in the next, and so on, though in a new way. The highest level, the Root or the Source, creates and controls the events through all the worlds, down to the "branches" in our world.

THE SAME BUT OPPOSITE

To indicate the difference in the quality of the substance in each world, the same elements in each world receive different names. The Upper World, for instance, contains angels, while our world contains animals. This does not mean that animals are angels. But if we keep in mind the world within a world concept from the previous chapter, we will recall that each element in reality contains five levels: 0–4. Level 3 of the will to receive in the spiritual world is called "angels," and the same level in the physical world is called "animals."

The correspondence between the Upper and lower systems is similar to having an object, which you can sink in wax, in sand, in plaster, in cement, or in dough. The final result is different because of the different substances. The shape, however, is the same. Even though the quality of the matter or its behavior is different, the final form corresponds to the shape that made it.

Tidbits

Kabbalah explains that at the end of correction, when all our desires are corrected, even the angel of death will become a holy angel. It means that when we are corrected we will see that all the forces we thought were evil are actually good but presented themselves as evil to prompt us to correct.

But the matter is always opposite than the shape. If you press a flat board with a little dome in the middle against the beach sand, you will get a flat surface with a little crater in it. Similarly, the Creator is the shape and we are the matter. Because He is a giver, we are receivers.

Just like the dome and the crater, our will to receive is the exact negative of His desire to give. It contains all the elements that exist in Him, but in an inverted way: what's good in Him is bad in us. And since He is only good, we are only ... you get the point.

THE HIDDEN MEANING
OF THE BIBLE

The Bible (or Torah) is sublime and spiritual, but, frankly, it can be a bit long on history with its lists of relations. You read about people marrying, divorcing, cheating on each other, and killing one another. A fair question might be: what's so spiritual about that?

In the framework of Kabbalah, however, the Bible doesn't tell stories of people. Instead, it presents relations between spiritual forces.

The Bible shows the process of the correction of souls through higher forces. This takes the souls on their path of ascent as they rise in their ability to bestow. Characters such as Adam, Noah, and Abraham are not thought of as people who lived somewhere and wandered (or floated) around. They are considered forces that operate over desires that have to be corrected, within each and every one of us. For example, the story of the exodus of Hebrew slaves from Egypt represents not their freedom from physical bondage, but the acquisition of the first *Masach* (screen), the crossing of the barrier.

Spiritual Sparks

First, you must know that when dealing with spiritual matters that have no concern with time, space, and motion, and especially when dealing with Godliness, we do not have the words by which to express and contemplate. ...For that reason, the sages of the Kabbalah have chosen a special language, which we can call "the language of the branches."

—Baal HaSulam, *The Study of the Ten Sefirot*

Some stories may seem to have no rationality or sanctity in them. When reading them, remember that these are not events, but stories of forces. They are not to be understood or justified in earthly terms.

BEHIND THE MONITOR

The Language of the Branches is the expression of higher forces that operate on our world. It is expressed in objects and in everything that happens. Where does it come from? It's like a computer monitor: if you looked behind the monitor, you would not see the picture—you would see the electronics that built it.

> **Spiritual Sparks** ☺
>
> You have not a blade of grass below that has not a sign Above, which strikes it and tells it, "grow."
>
> —*Midrash Rabba*

Let's say there is a picture on the screen, a beach. Behind the screen is not a beach, but a collection of electric impulses, forces and energies that create the picture on the screen. The picture is the "branch," and the electric forces that create this picture are its "roots." The connection you have with the electronic forces (root) through the picture (branch) is called the Language of the Branches.

Here's how some of the stories in the Bible are explained using the Language of the Branches.

THE APPLE STORY

Let's talk about the Biblical story of creation. The will to receive in the common soul (us) is called "Eve." The will to bestow, to give, is called "Adam." Egoism—the will to receive with the intention to receive—is called "the serpent," and we call it "ego." The ego wants to take over all our desires and pull us toward egoism. This is considered that the serpent came to Eve—the will to receive—and said, "You know what? You can use your will to receive in a very good way." So Eve went to Adam—the will to bestow—and said, "You know what? We have a chance to climb up to the highest worlds here. Moreover, this is what the Creator wants, that's why He made us receivers."

And she ate. The will to receive, joined with the serpent (egoism), ate the apple. Because they liked it, they thought, "Why not pull Adam (the forces of bestowal) into it?" So she did. As a result, the whole body of *Adam ha Rishon* (the common soul), all his desires were corrupted by the serpent's intention to receive in what became the original sin.

ABRAHAM—BETWEEN EGYPT AND ISRAEL

Abram was born in Mesopotamia (today's Iraq), immigrated to Israel, and then, because of famine, went down to Egypt. This travel has a spiritual meaning because these places are degrees or forces. They actually tell the correction story of his desire.

Mesopotamia is a starting point, where Abram's desires are egoistic, like yours and mine. The land of Israel, called "desires to bestow," is the desire to give. Egypt is called *Malchut*, the will to receive, and it consists of egoistic desires, with Pharaoh being the epitome of egoism.

☺✍ **Tidbits**

In Kabbalah, Israel is not a piece of land. Its name comes from two words: *Yashar* (straight), *El* (God, Creator). Therefore, to a Kabbalist, anyone with a strong desire to be like the Creator is considered a part of Israel.

When Abram first achieved correction, he changed his name to Abraham, broken down as *Av* (father) *ha Am* (the nation)—the great desires to receive that were to emerge from him. To match those desires, he had a will to give, which guaranteed that the desires will ultimately be corrected. Every time Abraham increases his will to give, he moves to Israel, and every time he increases his will to receive, he moves to Egypt. This is also why immigration to Israel is considered ascent and immigration to Egypt is considered descent.

The will to give by itself is powerless. You can truly give to the Creator only by receiving from Him. So Abraham asked, "How will I know that I will reach the same level of giving as the Creator?" Abraham couldn't receive because he was in a state of giving. The Creator put his seed in Egypt and told him he would receive the full measure of the will to receive. Abraham was delighted. After the exile, when the people mingle with the Egyptians and absorb their desires, the people will be corrected and know how to receive in order to bestow. This is the pattern of attainment for everyone and leads to the end of correction.

The Bible says that Abraham went down to Egypt because of famine. The famine was spiritual because he wanted to bestow but had nothing to bestow with. For Abraham, a situation in which he can't bestow is called famine, absence of desires to receive. As a person gradually acquires a bigger will to receive, it is considered experiencing the exile in Egypt. When you come out of the experience with great substance of vessels of reception, you can begin to correct them so they work in order to bestow.

MOSES' TUG-OF-WAR WITH PHARAOH

The next key Bible story from the perspective of Kabbalah is the story of Moses. Pharaoh enslaving the Jews has deeper significance than historical record.

Pharaoh dreamed that there would be 7 years of wealth, followed by 7 years of famine. Wealth is when you first discover a great desire for spirituality and feel great happiness. This is because you think that you can achieve spirituality using your ego. You are ready to read and learn and do all kinds of things. Famine happens when you see that you cannot acquire spirituality unless you concede your ego and gain the attribute of giving. But you can't give, despite wanting to. You are caught in between. This is Egypt.

To bring about change, your "Pharaoh" grows. Your Pharaoh is your ego. It begins to show you bad things about the present state. If it is very bad, you want to escape or flee to spirituality. You want to go even if there is nothing appealing and attractive about it. When your ego shows you how bad it is, you will want to change.

The name Moses comes from the word *Moshech* (pulling). This is the point that pulls us out of Egypt, just like the Messiah, which also comes from the same word. Moses is the feeling within a person that stands against his or her ego and says, "I really think we should leave." The big force that pushes is Pharaoh. The small force that pulls is Moses. This pulling is the start of your spirituality, the point in the heart.

THE (CLASSIC HAPPY-END) STORY OF ESTHER

This story describes the final correction of the will to receive, named Haman. Mordechai (the will to bestow) and Haman share a horse. Haman rides first, then Haman lets Mordechai ride while he walks the horse. This shows how your will to receive ultimately surrenders before your will to bestow and gives up the reins.

Esther–from the Hebrew word *Hester* (concealment)–is the hidden Kingdom of Heaven. She is hidden, along with Ahasuerus, the Creator, who is seemingly neither good nor bad. The person who experiences it doesn't know who's right and whether the Creator is good or bad.

Esther is also a relative of Mordechai, the will to bestow. Mordechai, like Moses but at a different spiritual stage, is the point of *Bina* in one's soul, which pulls you toward the Light.

When the will to give appears, sometimes it cannot be seen right away. Sometimes it is hidden, like Esther the Queen. You may not know if the action is really giving. However, if Mordechai is the one riding, your will to receive can correct itself.

Tidbits

The happiest holiday in the Hebrew calendar is Purim, when the story of Haman and Mordechai is told. This holiday represents the end of correction, and dictates drinking until we cannot tell Haman from Mordechai, egoism from altruism. This is because at the end of correction, all desires are corrected and work in order to give to the Creator, so it doesn't matter which desire you work with, it'll always be with the intention to give.

THE ZOHAR—NOT WITHOUT ATTAINMENT

All that *The Zohar* speaks of, even its legends, are the 10 *Sefirot—Keter, Hochma, Bina, Hesed, Gevura, Tifferet, Netzah, Hod, Yesod,* and *Malchut*—and their interactions. To a Kabbalist, the entries and their various combinations are sufficient to reveal all the spiritual worlds.

Rabbi Shimon Bar-Yochai (Rashbi), author of *The Zohar,* had a big problem. He was debating with himself on how to convey Kabbalah knowledge for future generations. He did not want to expose people to the content in *The Book of Zohar* prematurely. He was afraid this would only confuse and mislead people from the true path.

To avoid confusion, he entrusted the writing in the hands of Rabbi Aba, who knew how to write in a special way so only the worthy would understand. Because of *The Zohar's* special language, only those who are *already* on the ladder of spiritual degrees understand what is written there. *The Zohar* is only for those who've already crossed the barrier and acquired some level of spirituality. They are the ones who can understand the book, according to their spiritual degree.

Today, most souls are too materialistic and egoistic to understand *The Zohar*. They need tools to bring them into the spiritual "zone" first. It's like a space shuttle that needs a big thrust before it can continue on its own engine. A supportive environment, teacher, and correct books give your spiritual understanding a "boost."

There are different styles of writing in *The Zohar*. It was written in different languages, depending on how they wanted to express specific spiritual states. Sometimes the various languages create confusion. When the book talks about laws, people may think *The Zohar* is preaching morals. When it tells stories, people may see them as fables. Without spiritual attainment, it is difficult to understand what *The Zohar* is really about.

Some of *The Zohar* is written in the language of Kabbalah, and some of it is written in the language of legends. Below are examples of two such legends.

THE DONKEY DRIVER

The Zohar contains a beautiful story about a donkey driver, a man who drives the donkeys of important men so they can carelessly walk and talk about their affairs. But the donkey driver in *The Zohar* is a force that helps a person who already has his own soul.

In the story, two men talk about spiritual matters as they walk along from one place to another. Whenever they come to a dilemma they can't resolve, the donkey driver "miraculously" gives them the answer. As they progress (thanks to the driver's answers), they discover that their simple donkey driver is actually a heaven-sent angel who is there for just that purpose: to help them progress. When they have progressed to the final degree, they find that their driver is already there, waiting for them.

The Kabbalistic interpretation: the donkey is our will to receive, our egoism. You and I all have a donkey driver, waiting for us to enter the spiritual world so he can guide us. But just like the legend, we will discover who the donkey driver really is only when we reach his degree, at the end of our correction.

THE NIGHT OF THE BRIDE

Before the end of correction, there is a special state called "the night of the bride." The story in *The Zohar* talks about the preparation of the bride for the wedding ceremony. The bride is the collection of all the souls. It is a *Kli* that is ready to bond with the Creator.

When you reach this state, you feel that your *Kli* is prepared, supported, and ready for spiritual unity. The groom is the Creator. It is called "night" because the *Dvekut* (unity) is still not apparent and the Light is still not shining in the vessels. Night means that the vessels still feel darkness, absence of unity.

When the night turns into day, the abundance of the end of correction is promised, but *The Zohar* doesn't tell us exactly why it is good—only that it is wholeness, Light, and peace.

THE BEGINNING OF THE LAST GENERATION

The writing of *The Tree of Life* by the Ari, marks the beginning of the last phase in the evolution of the souls. The Ari writes that his phase is the last generation. From his time on, the wisdom of Kabbalah begins to emerge from hiding, though it still takes centuries. With him, a new *qualitative* process has begun.

Kabbalist writers can feel that their phase is the last before correction because they know it takes only a little *MAN* (prayer for correction) to reveal everything and put an end to our world's troubles. There's just a fraction of an inch missing to make contact. Crossing the gap is up to us, and this is why Kabbalists try to spread their knowledge, so more souls are corrected. They feel we are very close to completing our correction.

THE STUDY OF THE TEN SEFIROT

The words of Rabbi Shimon Bar-Yochai were written in *The Book of Zohar* by his student, Rabbi Aba. The words of the Ari were written by his student, Chaim Vital. But unlike his spiritual ancestors, Rav Yehuda Ashlag, known as Baal HaSulam (Master of the Ladder) for his *Sulam* (ladder) commentary on *The Book of Zohar*, wrote his books by himself.

The "flagship" of his work is his commentary on the writings of the Ari, known as *Talmud Eser Sefirot* (*The Study of the Ten Sefirot*). In six volumes and more than 2,000 pages, Baal HaSulam explains to uneducated souls of the twentieth and twenty-first centuries what the Ari actually meant when he wrote *The Tree of Life*. Baal HaSulam wrote his book specifically to people who want spirituality and nothing else. In his "Introduction to The Study of the Ten Sefirot," he states that his intended audience is those who ask, "What is the meaning of my life?"

IN A NUTSHELL

- All things in this world are branches of roots that first appear in the spiritual world.
- The Bible is written in the language of the branches, using worldly names and terms to indicate spiritual processes.
- The stories of the Bible and *The Zohar* are not about people—they are about forces that act on souls.
- The book written with our correction in mind is *The Study of the Ten Sefirot* and its author is Baal HaSulam.

10
WHEN LETTERS AND WORDS ADD UP

JUST THE GIST
- Getting a handle on Hebrew letters, words, and numbers
- The Creator-creation-desire connection
- The way numbers, words, and letters reflect your own correction

The Hebrew language, and the way it is written, is a direct result of communication with the Upper Worlds. The combination of letters and the strokes of ink that make them up are laced with spiritual knowledge.

Also, letters, words, and numbers are usually three separate things, but they are intricately linked in Kabbalah. Understanding their relationship gives greater spiritual meaning to each of them. Each letter and the words that they form have their own spiritual story to tell, so let's begin telling them.

THE TIES BETWEEN LETTERS, WORDS, AND NUMBERS

In Hebrew, each letter corresponds to a number. As a result, any word or name can become a series of numbers. Numbers can be taken one at a time or added together. Its letters are results of spiritual sensations. The direction of the lines and shapes in a letter has spiritual meaning.

As a result, Hebrew letters are also codes for sensations the writer receives from the Creator. When a letter or word is written, the author is giving us his or her conscious perception of the Creator. The Creator is acting on them as they write.

The color in writing is also a clue to the way creation (black ink) works hand in hand with the Creator (white paper). Without both of them, you could not understand the writing or the story of creation and what it means to you.

A MAP OF SPIRITUALITY

The *Torah* is the major text of Judaism and the "Old Testament" in Christianity, as well as a Kabbalah text. Believe it or not, this large book in its original form was recorded as a single word. Later, this single word was divided into more words, which are made of letters.

The letters show all the information that is radiating down from the Creator. There are two basic kinds of lines in Hebrew letters, representing two kinds of Light. The vertical lines stand for the Light of wisdom or pleasure. The horizontal lines stand for the Light of mercy, or correction. (There are also diagonals and circular lines that have specific meanings in each letter, but that's beyond the scope of this book.)

The codes come from changes in the Light as it develops your *Kli* (desire). The Light expands your desire. When Light enters your *Kli*, it is called *Taamim* (flavors), and when it leaves, it is called *Nekudot* (dots or points). Memories of Light entering are called *Tagin* (tags), and memories of Light departing are *Otiot* (letters).

All letters start with a dot or point. A complete cycle of a spiritual state contains entrance, departure, memories of the entrance, and the memories of the departure. The fourth and last element creates letters, and the other three are written as tiny symbols *Taamim* (flavors), tags (*Tagin*), and dots (*Nekudot*) above, within, and below the letters respectively.

With correct instruction for reading the *Torah*, Kabbalists can see their past, present, and future states by gazing at these symbols in each of their combinations. But to see that, it is not enough to simply read the text. You must know how to see the codes.

Certain combinations of letters can be used instead of the language of *Sefirot* and *Partzufim* when you describe spiritual actions. Objects and actions shown through letters and their combinations, too, can give a description of the spiritual world.

The key to reading the *Torah* in this way is *The Zohar*. In essence, the book contains commentaries on the five parts of the *Torah* and explains what is concealed in the text of Moses.

The letters represent information about the Creator. More precisely, they describe the individual's experience of the Creator. Kabbalists depict the Creator as white Light, the background of the paper on which letters and words are written. The creature's perceptions of the Creator emphasize different sensations that a person feels while experiencing the Creator, using letters and words. This is why traditional Hebrew writing is made of black letters over a white background.

It turns out that the Hebrew letters are like a map of spirituality, describing all the spiritual desires. The way they connect gives us the *Torah*.

DOTS AND LINES

The dots and lines in Hebrew letters are shapes on the paper, which is blank and void. The paper is the Light, or Creator. The black ink on it is the creation.

A vertical line (|) means that the Light descends from Above—from the Creator toward creation. A horizontal line (−) means the Creator is relating to all existence (like the sweep of a landscape).

The shape of Hebrew letters comes from the combination of *Malchut* (represented by black) and *Bina* (represented by white). The black point is *Malchut*. When the dot connects to the Light, it expresses the way it receives the Light through all kinds of forms and shapes. The shapes show the different ways creation (black ink) reacts to the Creator (the white background).

Each letter signifies combinations of forces. Their structure and how letters are pronounced express qualities of the Creator. You express the spiritual qualities you achieve through the shapes.

BLACK ON WHITE

Hebrew letters also represent *Kelim* (vessels). *The Zohar* tells us that the letters appeared one by one before the Creator and asked to be selected to serve Him in creating the universe. Put simply, the letters asked to receive his blessing and give it to creation, just as a *Kli* (vessel) receives water and pours it out to sustain life.

White symbolizes Light (giving) and black symbolizes darkness (receiving). For this reason, the properties of the Creator are absolutely white, symbolized by the white paper. Black is creation, symbolized by the black ink. Alone, the Creator and creation cannot be understood at all. Together, they make letters and symbols that can be read and understood.

Think of it this way: without a creation, can we really call the Creator, "Creator"? To be a Creator, He needs to create. This Creator-creation dualism is the basis for all that exists. You can talk about something only from the perspective of the being that perceives that something.

Off Course

Even if we take the subtlest word that can be used ... the word "Upper Light" or even "Simple Light," it is still borrowed and lent from the light of the sun, or candlelight, or a light of contentment one feels upon resolving some great doubt. ...How can we use them in context of the spiritual and Godly? ... It is particularly so where one needs to find some rationale in these words to help one in the negotiation customary in the research of the wisdom. Here one must be very strict and accurate using definitive descriptions ...

—Baal HaSulam,
"The Essence of the Wisdom of Kabbalah"

The shapes of the letters symbolize a connection and bond between you and the Creator. They are not just black lines; they form clear shapes because they represent corrected relationships between creation and Creator.

This bond is built on contrast and collision. As creatures, you and I don't experience Light unless it collides with something. To sense Light, it must be stopped by something, such as the retina in your eye. The surface of an object (sound, light, or any kind of wave) collides with our perception. This stops it from continuing and allows us to sense it.

Because the paper is like the Light, it must be stopped with black lines (letters). That allows a person to sense the Light and learn from it. The black lines of the letters are seen as a barrier to the Light. This is because black (the color) is the opposite of Light. The Light strikes against the creature's *Masach*; it wants to enter the *Kli* and give delight. Instead of deflecting it, the struggle between the rejecting *Masach* and the striking Light creates a powerful bond. This collision is what the relationship between the Light and letters is based on.

In this way, the black lines of the letters limit the Light or restrict it. When the Light "hits" a line, it is forced to stop, and then the *Kli* can study it. It turns out that the only way to learn anything about the Creator is by stopping His Light—restricting it and studying it. Ironically, it is precisely when you contain the Creator that you learn how to be as free as Him. In a sense, the *Masach* is like a prism: the rejection of Light breaks it into the elements that comprise it, and this allows us, creatures, to study it and decide how much of each "color" we want to use.

LETTERS AND WORLDS

Hebrew consists of 22 letters. The first nine letters, *Aleph* through *Tet*, represent the lower part of *Bina*. The next nine, *Yod* through *Tzadik*, stand for *Zeir Anpin*, and the last four, *Kof* through *Tav*, stand for *Malchut*, the creature itself.

On Course

You study the qualities of the Creator in the same way you determine an object's color. When you see a red ball, it means that the ball reflected the red color, and that's why we can see it. Similarly, when you reject (reflect) a fragment of the Creator's Light, you know exactly what you rejected. This is why the only way you can know the Creator is by first rejecting all His Light. Then you can decide what you want to do with it.

In addition to the "regular" letters, there are five final letters in Hebrew. If you look at the illustration on the following page, you will see that they are not new letters; they bear the same names as letters in the original 22. There is a good reason for that.

The original 22 letters are all in the world of *Atzilut*, the highest of the five worlds introduced in Chapter 7. Because the original 22 letters are in the world closest to the Creator, they describe a corrected connection between creation and Creator. The five final letters

א = Aleph	1	י = Yod	10	ק = Kof	100
ב = Bet	2	כ = Chaf	20	ר = Reish	200
ג = Gimel	3	ל = Lamed	30	ש = Shin	300
ד = Dalet	4	מ = Mem	40	ת = Tav	400
ה = Hey	5	נ = Nun	50		
ו = Vav	6	ס = Samech	60		
ז = Zayin	7	ע = Ain	70		
ח = Het	8	פ = Peh	80		
ט = Tet	9	צ = Tzadik	90		

Final Letters:

ך = Final Chaf	20
ם = Final Mem	40
ן = Final Nun	50
ף = Final Peh	80
ץ = Final Tzadik	90

The Hebrew Letters and Their Numeric Values

make contact between the corrected state (World of *Atzilut*) and the worlds of the uncorrected state, *Beria, Yetzira, Assiya* (BYA). Because there are five phases in creation, there must be five final forms of contact between *Atzilut* and BYA, hence the five final letters.

The letter *Bet* is the first letter in the *Torah* and the second letter in the Hebrew alphabet. It's the first in the *Torah* because *Bet* stands for the corrected connection between *Bina* and *Malchut*, which is called *Beracha* (blessing). A blessing is received when *Malchut* (creation, us) can connect to *Bina* (Creator). We can connect to Him *only* when we want to be like Him, and that's what is meant by "corrected connection." When *Malchut* asks to be like *Bina*—that is, when you and I want to be like the Creator—it is called "a corrected connection" blessing (*Beracha*).

ONES, TENS, HUNDREDS, AND BEYOND

Letters are divided into three numerical categories: ones, tens, and hundreds:

- The *Bina* level corresponds to ones: *Aleph, Bet, Gimel, Dalet, Hey, Vav, Zayin, Het, Tet*. These are the nine (1–9) *Sefirot* of *Bina*.
- The *ZA* level corresponds to tens: *Yod, Chaf, Lamed, Mem, Nun, Samech, Ayin, Peh, Tzadik*. These are the nine (10–90) *Sefirot* of *ZA*.
- The *Malchut* level corresponds to hundreds: *Kof, Reish, Shin, Tav*. These are the four (100–400) *Sefirot* of *Malchut*.

The obvious question comes to mind: what about the numbers above 400? The answer is that Hebrew is a spiritual language, not a math language. Everything about it represents spiritual states, and no more numbers are required to describe the structure of the world of *Atzilut* (the "home" of the letters). In other words, with these 22 letters, you can describe *everything* from the beginning of creation to infinity.

So what happens when you want to express complicated numbers, like 248? You use three letters: *Reish* (200), *Mem* (40), and *Het* (8). And what if you want to write a higher number than 400, like 756? You use more than three letters: *Tav* (400) + *Shin* (300) + *Nun* (50) + *Vav* (6) = 756.

Of course, we can reach this number using many different combinations, but it is important to remember that if two words add up to the same number, they are spiritual synonyms and have the same spiritual meaning.

Now here's how this discussion of numbers relates to the evolution of spiritual desire explained in Kabbalah. When numbers represent the size of your *Kli*, the bigger they are, the more Light enters them. If there are only ones in your desire, that is, if you have a small desire, a small amount of Light is present. If tens are added and your desire grows, more Light enters. If hundreds are added and your desire reaches its peak, the Light symbolized by the letters fills your spiritual *Kelim*.

Things get tricky, however, as Kabbalah has an exception. Numbers can also represent the Light, not just the desires. In this case, ones (small Lights) are in *Malchut*, tens are in ZA, and hundreds are in *Bina*. This is because of an inverse relation between Light and *Kli* (desire). This may be confusing, but it is because the greatest Light of the Creator enters your *Kli* only when you activate your lowest desires.

Here are the numerical values of each level expressed in terms of the Light they represent and the level at which they fill your vessels:

- **Bina**—Light (100); *Kli* (1)
- **ZA**—Light (10); *Kli* (10)
- **Malchut**—Light (1); *Kli* (100)

IF GOD = NATURE, AND NATURE = DESIRE, THEN...

Here's something else to think about: if you sum up the numeric values of the letters in the words *HaTeva* (the nature), they add up to 86. Next, if you sum up the value of the letters in the word *Elokim* (God), they add up to 86. And finally, if you sum up the value of the letters in the word *Kos* (cup), they add up to—you guessed it—86. That shows the equivalence of God, cup, and nature in Kabbalah, which we noted in Chapter 2. Here's how it works.

We've already said that if two words add up to the same number, they have the same spiritual meaning. Therefore, the statement that Kabbalah is making here is very interesting (if a little complex):

- Nature and Creator are one and the same. The fact that we don't see them as such doesn't make it less true, just like the fact that we can't see bacteria with a naked eye doesn't stop them from affecting our bodies.
- A cup, in Kabbalah, stands for a *Kli*, meaning a desire to receive. Therefore, nature and our *Kli* are the same. Here, too, the fact that we don't sense it doesn't mean it isn't true, but the fact that they have the same value means that we have the opportunity to correct (change) our desires to match nature's structure.
- When we match our desires (*Kli*) with those of nature, we will also match them with the Creator (because nature and the Creator are synonyms). In simple words, when we equalize our *Kli* with nature, we will discover the Creator.

In terms of an equation, it looks like this: If A = B, and B = C, then A = C.

THE BUILDING-BLOCKS OF LIFE

The name of all these "games" Kabbalists play with letters and numbers is *Gematria*. Ancient Kabbalists perfected *Gematria* to a point that they could (and did) describe the whole of creation and the Creator-creation relationship using *Gematria*, as the following sections demonstrate.

Gematria is an expression of the state of a *Kli* that discovers the Creator. The *Kli* discovers Him within its own structure. The *Kli* is made of 10 *Sefirot*. These 10 *Sefirot* are divided into the tip of the letter *Yod*, and then the letters *Yod*, *Hey*, *Vav*, and *Hey* again. This four-letter structure is known as the *tetragrammaton* (in Greek), *HaVaYaH* (in Hebrew), and Yaweh or JHVH or Jehovah (in English).

The first *Sefira*, *Keter*, belongs to the tip of the *Yod*; the second *Sefira*, *Hochma*, to the *Yod*; and the third *Sefira*, *Bina*, to *Hey*. The next *Sefira*, *ZA*, contains six internal *Sefirot*: *Hesed*, *Gevura*, *Tifferet*, *Netzah*, *Hod*, and *Yesod*. All those *Sefirot* are contained in the letter *Vav*. And the last *Hey* is *Malchut*, which is also the last *Sefira*.

Tidbits

We already said that there is no bad in Kabbalah; it's all a question of how we relate to the situations we're in. Pharaoh is considered an evil force. But Kabbalists inverted the Hebrew letters of the name Pharaoh, and found that it really meant *Oref H* (the posterior side of the Creator). In other words Pharaoh is really the Creator, harshly goading you to progress to spirituality because you are not pushing yourself hard enough. If you push harder, you will find that Pharaoh is really your friend.

As a matter of fact, *HaVaYaH* isn't just the structure of one *Kli*; it is the structure of every *Kli*—and of everything there is, was, or will be. It is the building-blocks of existence. Like a hologram, however small you cut it, you'll always get a structure of 10 complete *Sefirot*, contained in *HaVaYaH*. This is also why these four letters comprise the word *havayah* (a generic term that in Hebrew means existence, being).

ABRAHAM TOOK IT PERSONALLY (AND SO CAN YOU)

It's important to understand that there is a relationship between the letters, *Sefirot*, and the *Kli* because, in Kabbalah, a person's name stands for a person's spiritual *Kli*. Abraham, for instance, stands for a very specific kind of relationship between the Creator and creation. Abraham stands for a soul that made a certain kind of correction. When he was born, his name was Abram. But after he made the correction of turning his desires from egoistic to altruistic, he changed his name to Abraham. The added *h* stands for adding the *Hey* of *Bina* to his name, the Creator's quality of altruism. This indicates that he has risen to that spiritual level.

DISCOVER YOUR ROOT, DISCOVER YOUR NAME

All the letters exist within us and nowhere else. They are spiritual *Kelim*, experiences that each of us has felt and will feel again, as we develop in spirituality.

The *Kelim* perceive the Creator and when we learn the true meaning of the letters, we find within us all the lines, dots, and circles that symbolize our connection with the spiritual world. Every person has something called "the root of the soul." As we climb the spiritual ladder and discover the letters, words, and numbers within us, we gradually come closer to our true selves.

The Creator created only one creation. This creation was divided into 600,000 pieces, which then broke into the billions of souls we have in the world today. As we climb the ladder, we realize that we are one body, and we find our place in it. This is the root of our soul.

Each root has its own name, and when we reach the root of our soul, we discover our place in the system of creation and who we really are. And we describe it with a name that is just our own.

IN A NUTSHELL

- Hebrew letters describe a Kabbalist's relationship with the Creator.
- Hebrew letters carry numeric values. Similar numeric values indicate spiritual similarity, and identical values indicate spiritual synonymy.
- God = nature, and nature = desire (*Kli*). Hence, God = desire.
- As you climb the spiritual ladder, you discover the letters within you according to your spiritual state. This is how you discover your own true name.

11

BODY AND SOUL

JUST THE GIST

- The Kabbalah explanation of reincarnation
- The meaning of the body in the eyes of the soul
- The longest dinner party
- Soul Q&A's

Reincarnation is usually thought of as an event where a person lives and dies several times. But the notion of being reborn into a different identity is not the only form of reincarnation. In Kabbalah, a reincarnation is every time you make a step in spiritual growth. For example, if you correct yourself intensely, you can experience many lifetimes in a matter of minutes. On the other hand, when you go on without correcting yourself, you may never experience a single incarnation. This is how reincarnation is defined according to Kabbalah.

YOUR BODY—A CONTAINER FOR YOUR SOUL

Kabbalah recognizes people by spiritual characteristics. When Kabbalistic texts say a new person is created, they're not talking about arms and legs. They mean aims and desires. When the quality of your desires is transformed for the better, you would say, from a Kabbalistic perspective, that a new person, a more spiritual you, was created. The body is merely a biological container. Organs, for example, can be replaced through transplants. Kabbalah sees the body as a vehicle through which your soul can work. To correct your soul, your body must be present and active.

Spiritual Sparks

This life is not eternal ... for itself; it is rather like a sweat of life.

—Baal HaSulam, "Introduction to The Tree of Life"

Souls have only one desire while existing within physical bodies. They wish to return to their source, the level they were at prior to their descent. Your physical body, with its desire to receive, pulls the souls back into this world. Your desire to be spiritual helps your soul return to its spiritual roots.

RECYCLE UNTIL YOU'RE RIPE AND READY

Souls come down to earth and then up again in a cycle. They join bodies, return to the Source—another Kabbalistic term for the Creator—and repeat the process. They keep returning until they complete their correction.

You experience many incarnations, or new souls, in several ways. It can be through a troubling experience that makes you ready to question your purpose or seek new answers. It can be through Kabbalah study. When you are ripe for spirituality, for example, you may discover *A Guide to the Hidden Wisdom of*

Kabbalah. This book can be the beginning of your conscious incarnations.

The incarnations that flow through you then return to the Source. Your "task" on Earth is to go through as many incarnations as possible so that your soul finds ultimate correction.

WHY THE REPEATED APPEARANCES?

Reincarnation is the repeated appearances of souls within the bodies in this world. This occurs until each soul reaches its individual end of correction.

Complete correction is a multilevel undertaking—a soul may not complete its task and return to the Root in a single cycle. On its next entry, because of the progress you may have made, it reincarnates further along on the spiritual trail.

The Creator wants you to be filled with spiritual pleasure, to be complete. That is possible only through great desire. Only with a corrected desire can you reach the spiritual world.

We've already determined that a desire is considered corrected only when it has the right intention. This is not automatic; the "right intention" is acquired through study. This is a process, not an instant fix.

Today, by the way, the study itself isn't enough to get you to spirituality. You need a group of friends to support you, and you need to try to help others reach correction. This way you bond with their desire for spirituality (point in the heart), even when they are still unaware of it.

THE SEED OF THE SOUL

The purpose of your soul's correction is more than just for its own needs. The picture is much bigger! The correction of your soul affects all souls because all souls are connected. When you first come into this world, your soul is called a "point." Recall that we are all parts of one spiritual vessel or *Kli*, called

Adam ha Rishon (the First Man). Recall also that the soul of *Adam ha Rishon* was split into 600,000 souls, which come down to this world. This world occupies a large number of bodies, each with its own soul.

If you do not build a spiritual *Kli* out of this point while living here in this world, your soul returns to its root in *Adam ha Rishon*. It is like a seed that did not evolve, unconscious and lifeless. The goal is for you to return to the exact same root in *Adam ha Rishon* from which you came down.

WHERE AND WHAT IS A SOUL?

Location, as you and I think of it in time and space, does not exist in the Upper Worlds. What happens when the soul goes back to the Source? Actually, the soul returns to its root in *Adam ha Rishon*. "Root of the soul" is the place of the soul in the system of *Adam ha Rishon*. This is a spiritual location that is very close to the Source, the Creator. You cannot find this spiritual location with the five physical senses.

A soul is a spiritual force. In Kabbalah, souls are arranged in a pyramid, stacked according to their desires. Earthly desires are at the bottom, and spiritual desires are at the very top.

At the base of the pyramid are many souls with small desires (food, sex, sleep, and shelter). These are animal-like desires. The next level has those that desire wealth, something beyond basic needs. At the next level is the desire to control others, through power. Even fewer souls are here. Next is knowledge—these souls are

On Course

Kabbalists distinguish between what they call "the animate soul" and "a soul." The animate soul is what we're all born with: character, likes and dislikes, emotions, and tendencies. But when Kabbalists speak of a soul, they are referring to something quite different: a will to receive, corrected with a *Masach* that enables it to receive in order to give to the Creator.

engaged in discovery. At the top of the pyramid are the few souls that strive for attainment of the spiritual world. All these levels make up the pyramid.

This pyramid is also within you. You have the potential to act in all these ways. The pressure of the lower worlds must give way to the purest desire, the infinite desire for truth. Here you prefer to put effort and energy into increasing your desire for spirituality, rather than into earthly, egoistic desires. You don't have to do it all yourself—it is achieved through study, with groups, and through spreading the knowledge to others.

A SHIRT FOR THE SOUL

The body is the cover for the soul. You can think of your body as a shirt for the soul. Your soul connects you to all the other souls and to the Upper World, and this connection remains after your biological body is gone.

If you cultivate your altruism and think more about the unity of humanity and less about yourself, your efforts become a spiritual *Kli*. A *Kli* perceives the spiritual world, beyond your five senses. You feel the Upper Force in your soul, not in your body.

When spiritual perception is attained, you do not feel the physical life and death. This is because your soul is in the spiritual realm. By focusing on the development of your soul, you can

Spiritual Sparks

In our world, there are no new souls the way bodies are renewed, but only a certain amount of souls that incarnate on the wheel of transformation of the form, because each time they clothe a new body and a new generation.

Therefore, with regard to the souls, all generations since the beginning of Creation to the end of correction are as one generation that has extended its life over several thousand years, until it developed and became corrected as it should be. And the fact that in the meantime each has changed its body several thousand times is completely irrelevant, because the essence of the body's self, called "the soul," did not suffer at all by these changes.

—Baal HaSulam, "The Peace"

transcend biological (earthly) influences to the point that you are unaffected by them.

Rav Baruch Ashlag used to say that, to a Kabbalist, death and rebirth are as meaningless as taking your dirty shirt off and putting on a clean one. When his father, Rav Yehuda Ashlag, was asked where he wanted to be buried, he muttered in blatant indifference: "I couldn't care less where you dump my bag of bones."

NO TIME IN SPIRITUALITY

Time is our perception of the changes we experience as our soul develops. When your thoughts and desires change slowly, you feel that time is "crawling." When they change quickly, you feel that time is "flying."

Time is sensed only when we experience change. When your spiritual void is full, there are no changes. This is why it is said that there is no time in spirituality.

SOME Q&A's

All the souls on Earth have been here on previous occasions. It is like a dinner party where the guests keep going in and out. Each time they return, they learn something, leave, then bring it to the next party, which is held in a new house (person). All their experiences from past parties are applied to their present visit. Also, each time a soul visits, its desires strengthen and evolve because of its development in yesterday's party (life).

WHO WAS I?

Baal HaSulam writes in the article "The Freedom" that each generation contains the same souls as the previous generation, but in new bodies. The soul that is joined with your body could have been in a variety of persons, but there is no way to know because your soul is focused only on the present.

All of your memories are connected to one another. Everything you have ever experienced remains within you; nothing ever disappears. However, you cannot use it like a filing cabinet and pull out specific thoughts. Past memories appear on their own, in order to understand the present.

All souls are connected within the common soul of *Adam ha Rishon*. Because they are connected, memory is shared. Like a drop of water in a bucket, souls don't keep their earthly identities.

CAN WE IDENTIFY PEOPLE FROM THE PAST?

Yes we can. People's souls return to Earth. Kabbalists see the same soul reincarnated in Adam, Abraham, Moses, Rabbi Shimon, the Ari, and Yehuda Ashlag (all Kabbalist writers). It is as if the same soul covers itself in a contemporary Kabbalist each time it appears in our world. This allows each generation to get to know Kabbalah in its unique way.

However, Baal HaSulam was not born with the soul of the Ari. He was born and lived in his body as everyone does, with his own spiritual potential. In addition, though, he received the potential, the Light, the quality of bestowal called "Ari." This is the spiritual force of the Ari. He then continued developing it with the method of Kabbalah.

You, too, can try to have all the souls joined within you. In that state, you will have other souls beyond your own. One of these additional souls will be called "the donkey driver," the soul that helps steer you along your spiritual path, which we mentioned in Chapter 9.

On Course

When Kabbalah speaks of a person being in this world, it is referring to a person's will to receive in a state of concealment from the Creator, with no intention to give to Him. In other words, before we cross the barrier we are in this world. After we cross it we are in the next world.

CAN I REINCARNATE AS AN ANIMAL?

As far as souls are concerned, Kabbalah distinguishes between animals and humans. Animals are animate, while humans are both animate and spiritual. As humans, you and I have the ability to give back to the Creator.

The book, *Together Forever*, tells the story of a lonely magician who creates things to keep him company. He creates a dog, which is very loyal and good to care for, but the dog cannot reciprocate the specific care the magician gave.

Being able to reciprocate to the Creator is the gift of humanity. Therefore, reincarnation and evolution of souls deals only with human bodies.

> **Spiritual Sparks**
>
> Reincarnation occurs in all the objects of the tangible reality, and each object, in its own way, lives eternal life.
>
> —Baal HaSulam, "The Peace"

HOW MANY TIMES DO I HAVE TO REINCARNATE?

In his article, "Which Degree Should One Achieve?" Rav Baruch Ashlag—Yehuda Ashlag's son and a great Kabbalist in his own right—asks, "What is the degree one should achieve, so he will not have to reincarnate?" He answers that the soul continues to come back until it completes its correction and returns to its root. You don't have to correct anybody else, but you should try to give them the means to do it. If you've corrected yourself entirely, and did all you could for others, you will not continue to reincarnate.

The number of souls in the universal system is 600,000, and it is unchanging. There are 6,000 years given for all souls to reach attainment. As of 2009, there are 231 years left.

How long the souls continue to come back to Earth depends on how much progress is made toward their correction. You can think of it as your soul being on a journey, and you are the trail guide. If you lead the hikers (souls) to their goal, they won't have to come back next year to Trail Life, or they will come back stronger and ready to progress more. Any progress is good progress.

The goal is to bring all the souls to the top of the spiritual mountain, where complete correction is

Tidbits

A famous Chinese proverb says "Give a man a fish and you feed him for a day. Teach a man to fish and you feed him for a lifetime." This is similar to what we do when we help others to learn the knowledge of Kabbalah, which helps correct their souls.

achieved. They become more corrected as they climb. Until all souls reach the top, they will keep returning to our earthly bodies so we can help them climb. Studying Kabbalah speeds up the progress.

CAN I REMEMBER PAST LIVES?

You cannot sense past lives with your bodily senses. You have gone through phases in your life: baby, youth, teenager—all leading to you today. "You today" cannot see "you last week" because "you today" covered it up. All the phases are there, but you can see only the present state, "you today."

The most advanced point in your soul's past is your starting point in this life. If you achieve a high degree of spirituality, the next person that joins with your soul will have an even better starting point.

WHAT REMAINS OF PAST LIVES?

A previous life can also affect this one, usually positively. By simply existing, there is already some correction. This is because in every life cycle, we experience suffering. In that, we are no different from the rest of creation. This suffering leads to spiritual progress as we ask questions and seek change.

We can accelerate correction by making an effort to be spiritual. When we do, we feel pain consciously, and discover its cause. We then decide to change our intentions in order to get rid of the pain. This is how the past affects the present. This is important because there is a need to constantly renew the links between the souls. This fixes their connections in place and makes the unification of all the souls possible. This is called the correction of the collective soul.

Off Course

You *do not* want to progress through pain. This is not the way. Pain only leads you to thinking you're a martyr, making you proud and drives you away from the need to become like the Creator. The only good thing about pain is that it indicates that you are not in the right direction.

HOW CAN I POSITIVELY AFFECT MY NEXT LIFE?

The closer you bring your soul to the Creator in this life, the better off it will be in the next. With the correction you achieve, your soul will be "further along" spiritually in its next visit.

The closeness you achieve with the Creator in this life makes your soul's "return journey" easier in the next life because your soul is further along on the path to complete correction. People head toward correction either intentionally or by way of pain.

Everything you acquire (attributes, qualities, knowledge) in this world passes away except the changes in your soul. It's like a seed that will grow in the next rainy season. When the plant dies, its seed falls and sprouts another bud. What remains is the plant's energy. The spiritual energy that remains in us is a soul.

Kabbalah teaches that the ultimate measure of your life is in the difference between the soul you received at birth and the soul that you have now. This measures the extent to which you have spiritually elevated your soul.

IN A NUTSHELL

- Souls continue returning to Earth until they achieve complete correction.
- Reincarnation includes only the human soul, not the animate soul (character, likes and dislikes, emotions, and tendencies).
- The spiritual progress you've made in previous lives is your starting point in this one.
- If you want to know how you were, first discover who you *are* by discovering the root of your soul.
- You cannot change your species or even your gender between life cycles.

12

BECOMING A KABBALAH STUDENT

JUST THE GIST
- The shift from learning in dimly lit rooms to online open, free teaching
- Know which books to read for your spiritual progress
- Find the right teacher and learn how make the most of the study
- The power and practice of Kabbalah groups
- Kabbalah study online

The study of Kabbalah has changed dramatically over the years, and not just in the opening up of the once mysterious and secretive wisdom to the masses. Kabbalists are connected in the most technologically advanced and media-savvy ways. As a result, the books, teachers, and groups required to get the most out of Kabbalah study are easy to find today.

Today, you can go right to the authentic source texts of Kabbalah from your own home and in your own language. You can even find a teacher and a virtual group when you get to that point in your spiritual development. In this chapter, you learn how to use the study and live Kabbalah the modern way while staying true to the wisdom in the traditional texts.

EVERYDAY IS AN OPEN-HOUSE DAY

From the early Kabbalists, Adam and Abraham, through the writing of *The Zohar* and up to the Middle Ages, Kabbalah was primarily passed through word of mouth. Kabbalists primarily shared their spiritual experiences with each other as they discovered the Upper Worlds.

At the same time, Kabbalists prohibited the study of Kabbalah from people who had not been prepared for it. They treated their students cautiously, to ensure that they studied in the proper manner, and they intentionally limited the number of students.

Although we have made the point that Kabbalah study is open to all, we have not related how important the study of Kabbalah is today. To Kabbalists, in fact, wide dissemination of the wisdom of Kabbalah is a *must*. That, as much as anything else, accounts for the tremendous interest in Kabbalah today.

The reason why dissemination is a must is that Kabbalah is based on the need for all souls to correct, and places great importance on the collective. The greater the number of people studying Kabbalah, the greater the overall effect. When masses of people study, the quantity itself improves the quality of the study. Studying in the evening for half an hour or an hour is enough because millions, if not billions, of other people are doing the same. All of these people become spiritually connected, even if they don't feel it, and the mass has its effect on the entire world. Even tiny changes in millions of people produce great changes for the better in society as a whole (more on that in Part 3).

Spiritual Sparks

One learns in the place one's heart wishes.

—Ancient Kabbalists' maxim

As a result, today's method of Kabbalah study appeals to a mass audience, not just to a few ultra-dedicated students studying in the wee hours of the morning.

STUDYING WITH THE RIGHT INTENTION

Only two things are necessary to study Kabbalah correctly: a desire to improve your life and to find its meaning, and the right instruction. The right instruction is achieved by three means:

- The right books
- The right group
- The right teacher

A person who studies Kabbalah the right way, progresses without forcing him or herself. There can be no coercion in spirituality.

The aim of the study is to discover the connection between that student and what is written in the books. This is why Kabbalists wrote what they experienced and achieved. It is not to impart knowledge of how reality is built and functions, as in science. The purpose of Kabbalah texts is to create an understanding, assimilation, and sensation of the spiritual truth.

If a person approaches the texts in order to gain spirituality, the text becomes a source of Light, a correcting force. But if he or she approaches the texts in order to gain knowledge, the text will provide information, but nothing more. The measure of inner demand determines the measure of strength one gleans and the pace of one's correction.

If a person studies in the right manner, he or she crosses the barrier between this world and the spiritual world, entering a place of inner revelation. If the student does not achieve this, it is a sign of insufficient effort in either quality or quantity. It is not a question of the amount of study, but of the focus of the student's intentions. Of course, crossing the barrier doesn't happen overnight, but it should be the end result of the study.

Advancement in Kabbalah does not mean avoiding pleasures so that one's desire will not be kindled. Also, it is a mistake to believe that by being courteous and well-mannered you will achieve spirituality. Correction does not come from false pretense of correction.

NO COERCION IN SPIRITUALITY

The Kabbalah way absolutely rejects any form of coercion. If you experience any external pressure from others or any obligatory rules or regulations, it is a sign that the action is intended not by the Upper Worlds, but by someone's ego.

The study of Kabbalah enhances our desire for spirituality, bringing us to prefer it to materialism. Then, in relation to our spirituality, we clarify our desires. As a result, we either retreat from material things or not, depending on our attraction to or necessity for them.

On Course

Material desires appear successively, not all at once. If you felt a desire for money, it doesn't mean you won't feel it again tomorrow. You probably will, and even stronger. But the fact that desire for money appeared, disappeared, and reappeared is a sign you are working correctly, that the reappearance is a surfacing of a new *Reshimo*, from a new degree. It's a sign you completed your work on the previous degree and thus cleared the way for a new degree of desire to appear.

NO HERMITS

Kabbalah has changed not only in who can or cannot study, but also in its practices. As you'll recall from Chapter 5, some of the original Kabbalists, such as Rabbi Shimon Bar-Yochai, were essentially hermits. But even that was not because they chose that lifestyle; they were persecuted or forbidden to engage in Kabbalah. The Ari, for instance, was a rich merchant when he arrived as a Kabbalist in Safed. Kings David and Solomon also were neither poor nor hermits, as we all know, but they were great Kabbalists.

Rav Ashlag, for instance, believed in manual labor. When he came to Israel from Poland, he brought with him machines for processing leather. He wanted to start a leather factory, work during the day, and study at night. He also brought up his children in this manner. When his eldest son, Baruch Ashlag—who succeeded him—turned 18, Rav Ashlag sent him to work as a construction worker. He, too, would work during the day and study at night.

Yet there is a contradiction that anyone who follows Kabbalah faces. On one hand, earthly life is meaningless, and a serious Kabbalist ascribes no importance to it. On the other hand, it is a Kabbalah imperative to live within the flesh and feel it.

Tidbits

Why is Kabbalah traditionally studied before dawn, in the wee hours? When people sleep, the local "thought-field" is quieter, and there are fewer disturbances resulting from people's thoughts. Kabbalists also study in these hours because they have to work in the morning, just like everybody else. A true Kabbalist is forbidden to retire from worldly life.

Many teachings and religions in the world talk about abstinence. The more one diminishes one's corporal pleasures and the more one secludes oneself, the better it is for one's spiritual ascent. Kabbalah suggests the opposite: leave mundane and earthly things as they are, stop messing with your body and its habits, and deal only with the point in the heart. Rather than working to diminish your desires, Kabbalah suggests that you leave them alone, because restraining *physical* desires will not correct your *soul*.

THE TRINITY OF KABBALAH

Correction does not happen without study. For this reason, the Creator sent us the Trinity of Kabbalah: books, teachers, and groups of study companions. The rest of this chapter describes each of those tools of Kabbalah study—books, teachers, and groups—and you should work with them.

BOOKS: OUR SPIRITUAL TOUR GUIDES

Spirituality can be attained by studying the right books, meaning books written by a true Kabbalist. Reading the right books is like being led by a tour guide in a foreign country. With the aid of the guidebook, the traveler becomes oriented and better understands his new whereabouts.

We need books that are suited to our souls, books by the Kabbalists closest to our generation. This is because different souls descend in each generation, and each generation requires different teaching methods.

There is a special force in books of Kabbalah: any person who studies those books under the right guidance can attain the spiritual degree of the author. Students who follow the ways expounded by the writers of authentic books of wisdom can bond with the spiritual. By delving into a text of wisdom, they gradually rise to the spiritual level of the author.

Whenever you read the works of the righteous, you bond directly with them through the Surrounding Light (see Appendix). You are then enlightened, and your vessels of reception are purified and imbued with the spirit of the Creator.

Living in our world, we absorb various pictures and impressions. Because of that, we can all describe what we feel. But Kabbalah books describe experiences of a person who feels the spiritual world. They describe the writer's feelings of a world that most of us do not sense.

That is why Kabbalah books and Kabbalist writers are unique. A Kabbalist teacher is not only a person who feels the Upper World, but also a person who can describe emotions in a clear language so that others can feel and understand them. By studying books of Kabbalists, we nurture the missing senses within us, the ones that must be developed in order to feel the Upper World.

TEXTS IN THE LANGUAGE OF THE BRANCHES

There are many books of Kabbalah, written in various styles and forms, and written by Kabbalists in various degrees of attainment. This is why it is crucial that we know which books to study.

When a Kabbalist grasps spirituality, he feels it experientially, just as we experience the occurrences and incidences of this physical world with our physical senses and feelings. Because the objects in the spiritual realm are totally dissimilar from the objects of our physical world, it is difficult for Kabbalists to find the right words.

It happens in our world, too. We are not always able to explain our feelings, and at times we end up using vague words and gestures.

On Course

Don't become frustrated if what seemed clear yesterday becomes abstruse the next day. Depending on your mood and spiritual state when you are reading, the text can appear full of deep meaning or be entirely meaningless. Don't give up if the text appears to be vague, strange, or illogical. Kabbalah is studied to help you to see and to perceive, not for the sake of gaining technical knowledge.

This is why Kabbalah books are difficult to understand. Until we have a connection to spirituality, what we read is just words, without any understanding of the meaning behind them.

Remember, too, that Kabbalah uses the language of the branches, described in Chapter 9. The spiritual world and our own world are parallel. There is not an object, phenomenon, or force in this world that is not a consequence of the Upper World. Therefore, Kabbalists use names taken from our world in order to describe spiritual objects, for these objects are the roots of our world.

An ordinary person, as yet without a "spiritual screen," relates to books of Kabbalah as a kind of fairytale stories that happen in our world. But one who is already a Kab-balist is not confused by the words because he knows precisely which "branch" they stem from and which consequence in our world correlates to the "root" in the spiritual world.

Off Course

One of the most common mistakes beginners make is ascribing spiritual forces to branches, instead of focusing on the roots. For example, because we have a spiritual state called "water" (Hassadim, mercy), we also have water in our world. But that doesn't mean that if you drink water you become merciful.

BOOKS THAT HELP YOU REACH YOUR GOAL

Not all books, even authentic ones, have the same ability to promote you toward the spiritual world. Also, because Kabbalah has picked up many associations in its development (most of which are inaccurate, as described in Chapter 1), it is important to review the books you read with a thoughtful approach. Today, the same rule of caution applies to Internet sites.

To make this easy, most dedicated Kabbalists recommend abandoning all books on the subject of Kabbalah other than *The Zohar*, the writings of the Ari, and the writings of Baal HaSulam. That may be the best approach for the serious, lifelong Kabbalah student. For most anyone else, however, look for introductory books based on those writings, such as those listed in the Appendix. This book provides an introduction to the root sources so that readers can make enlightened choices for further study.

FINDING THE RIGHT TEACHER

But what is the correct way of studying and how do you make sure you study properly? Students who study correctly work on themselves and their inner beings, and they are guided by a teacher.

Experiencing the Creator requires a teacher. The teacher guides the student as the student rises to the spiritual level of the teacher and bonds with the teacher's wisdom and thoughts.

In fact, today, a single individual cannot enter the spiritual world. This would be like one individual beginning to develop the whole of physics or chemistry and then developing the technology to apply them. It would be similar to living like a Neanderthal without using all that humanity has achieved so far. In other words, it would be senseless.

That's why a beginning student needs a teacher who has already attained the Upper World and can show the student how to attain each step toward the Upper World. The teacher ushers the student into spirituality, but the student will fully understand the connection with the teacher only after attaining the Upper World independently.

Unity with the teacher occurs in the preliminary stages because both are on the worldly level. But unity with the Creator is possible only when you experience the Upper World. The teacher is your leader in that journey. Contact and unity with a teacher leads to contact and unity with the Creator.

LET YOUR HEART DECIDE

How do you find such a teacher? Kabbalah has a very simple answer: Study where your heart desires, where you feel you belong. The right teacher doesn't persuade you to think this or that. Kabbalah is a wisdom you learn of your own free will and choice. Spiritual development can take place in no other way.

When you detach yourself from persuasions, from anything external, from your upbringing, and from everything that you have heard in your entire life. When you feel in your heart that you have found a teacher and place of study, you should stay. That is the only valid test, and nothing else matters.

> **Spiritual Sparks**
>
> When I asked my teacher, Rav Baruch Ashlag, if he could prove he was the right teacher, Ashlag replied: "I have no answer for you. It is something you will have to answer in your own heart. You should believe no one. I do encourage you to go and look elsewhere, and if you find a better place for you, that's where you should stay."

As Rav Baruch Ashlag said, "Criticize and doubt everything. The most important objective is to be freed from prejudice, from education, and from public opinion. Free yourself from anything extraneous and try to absorb the way your nature tells you. That would be the truest, because any education and any external opinion is coercion."

> **Off Course**
>
> The teacher's role in Kabbalah is very subtle. The teacher must direct the student away from himself, and toward the Creator. There is no way a person can avoid the attention and admiration students shower on a teacher, unless the teacher has already transcended the ego and entered the Upper World. And how do you know your teacher is the right one? Let your heart decide!

GROUP STUDY

All of the great Kabbalists studied in groups. Rabbi Shimon Bar Yochai held a group of students, and so did the Ari. A group is vital in order to progress. It is the primary tool of Kabbalah, and everyone is measured by his contribution to the group.

A person who studies alone can use only one's own vessel to receive the Light of the Creator. Those who study in a group create a spiritual vessel that consists of all the participants, and everyone enjoys its illumination.

Also, in today's high-tech world, a group doesn't have to meet in a physical location. It can be a group of like-minded people who share a common (spiritual) goal, and they can meet on the Internet. Such a group can be contacted at this e-mail: info@kabbalah.info.

JOINT DESIRES

The group provides strength. Everybody has only a small desire for spirituality. The way to augment the will for spirituality is through joint desires. Several students together stimulate the Light and provide a unified force-field that is stronger as a whole than each individual on his or her own.

The reason is that we are all parts of the same soul (remember Adam?). Mixing the parts together recreates the collective vessel and brings us more Light. This Light affects each person in the group, and this way, all the group members become corrected both individually and as a collective.

A group is like a partnership. You can fall and have nothing left of the previous spiritual state, but the group will continue to exist and hold your desire for you. Your share in the group continues to exist, regardless of your present state.

LETTING THE LIGHT FLOW INTO YOU

Rav Yehuda Ashlag said that you must think of your group members as great (in spirituality). This will help you absorb spiritual powers from them when you are in personal decline. This is similar to the law of connected vessels, by which water always flows to the lowest place. If you think of the Light, or spiritual power, as water, then all you need to do is feel lower than your friends. The Light in them will flow into you, and as a result, more Light will flow into them from Above.

This creates continuous progress of the entire group. Although the group members may change roles according to their personal spiritual states, the group's progression is endless, and always toward enhanced spirituality.

How do you make the most of group study? This is done by a very simple means: you absorb from the group their appreciation for the goal of unification with the Creator. This is what the verse "Love thy friend as thyself" relates to; this is what makes them your friends.

If you listen to them, and if you appreciate your friends in the group, you will absorb the message of the greatness of the Creator, the greatness of bestowal. Then you can really become a group of Kabbalists.

On Course

The information in this book builds the foundations for your journey toward perceiving the spiritual forces of the Upper Worlds. Yet it is only the beginning. At later stages in your ascent, progress can be made only with the help of a teacher and a group, either in person or online.

LONG DISTANCE KABBALAH STUDY

Kabbalists are standing by ... it's almost like a call center these days. The general public cannot have a teacher standing next to each of them, but teachers are available to anyone, anywhere.

Advanced communications connect groups with teachers. Everything develops according to what is needed for the final correction; this is why communication has developed in the way it has. Social networks, e-learning, cheap and fast Internet, all those make Kabbalah study accessible to everyone.

Baal HaSulam, Rav Kook, and other great Kabbalists noted that the teaching must be suitable for today's world. The Internet offers an ideal way to study Kabbalah. You can watch live lessons or download them at your convenience. You can partake in online worldwide meetings and conferences of students, and a few times a year you can travel to regional gatherings of friends to enhance your connection with them. The Bnei Baruch site, for example, **www.kab.info**, offers all these online possibilities at no cost.

IN A NUTSHELL

- Kabbalah is not only open for everyone today, but disseminating it is the call of the hour.
- There is no coercion in spirituality; study where your heart desires.
- The Trinity of Kabbalah is the (right) books, the (right) teacher, and the (right) group.
- Today, learning with a virtual group is just as effective as learning with physical group.

13

LET THE MUSIC SPEAK

JUST THE GIST
- When words fail, music will prevail
- The two modes (and moods) of Kabbalistic music
- Music and the World to Come

Kabbalists have always written music as part of their spiritual expression. It's an inseparable part of their spirituality and stems directly from their spiritual degree.

Because there are no words in the spiritual Upper Worlds, music fills in where words fail. For a music-sensitive student, music can be just as beneficial and powerful as any book—at times, even more so.

NOT BY WORDS ALONE

Starting to perceive the Upper World, a Kabbalist enters a different dimension. An entire world is revealed before you in its full grandeur and wealth. It is something that does not exist in this world.

The Kabbalist perceives an entirely different picture: forces that bring our world into action and souls that are not attached to bodies. Past, present, and future stand before the Kabbalist in the present. The Kabbalist experiences all of this and lives fulfilled with the eternal, perfect sensation, a feeling that encompasses the whole universe.

> **Spiritual Sparks**
>
> When the lower ones begin their lives by song... the Upper Ones grant them more power so the lower ones will attain the Upper Light of Wisdom that has become revealed in ZON of the World of *Atzilut* and in the angels preceding it. This way, the lower ones increase the powers and luminescence of the wisdom in the Upper Realms.
>
> —Rav Yehuda Ashlag,
> *The Sulam Commentary on The Zohar*

Words are not enough to express this deep emotional experience. How do you describe something that can't be seen or touched? The worlds of Kabbalah have to be "felt" by the Kabbalist.

When words fail, music can provide insights beyond our common understanding. Music has the power to "move" us and to make us sense things that are beyond words.

MUSIC—TOUCHES WHERE TEXTS CAN NOT

Kabbalists use texts to explain to others the levels of spirituality they have reached. In their writings, however, Kabbalists only advise us on how to attain an impression, sensation, and discovery of this reality. They write about the kind of actions that you must perform within, with your desires, screens, and *Reshimot*—with everything inside your soul.

The books say, in effect, "Perform certain actions and you will discover certain things." They do not, however, describe what we will *feel* because it is impossible to convey the feeling in words.

It is similar to offering a new food to someone and saying, "Try it, and you'll see what it's like!" Whether it is bitter or sweet, you only hint at what the person is going to sense or how he will experience the sensation. Yet the sensation itself is experienced only by the person receiving the offer, not by anyone else.

This is why it is difficult for Kabbalists to convey what they feel, what they face, what is revealed before them: what the concealed world is like. Only one medium somehow expresses the impressions and delight of a person before whom the Upper World has revealed itself, and that is music. This is why, in addition to writing articles and very deep, intricate material, Kabbalists also write melodies and songs. It is one more way to express the sensations of a Kabbalist in a more concise manner, from heart to heart, through melodies, without words, so that these melodies would permeate our hearts and change us in some way, somehow tuning us into perceiving the Upper World.

Off Course

Even music cannot convey impressions of the Upper World precisely, for we do not have the same *Kelim* (vessels), the same sensory organs, or the same inner attributes as Kabbalists who attain and sense the Upper Worlds. Music gives us an impression of the Upper Worlds, a similar sensation yet a weak duplicate.

BATHING IN LIGHT

Kabbalah music expresses the spiritual states of the Kabbalist. The melodies are composed to describe the experience of two opposing stages in spirituality. The first is agony, a result of drifting away from the Creator. The feeling of drifting away from the Creator produces sad music, expressed by a prayer appealing for closeness. The second emotion is delight, felt as a result of getting closer to the Creator. This feeling of closeness to the Creator produces joyous music, expressed by a thanksgiving prayer. If you listen to Kabbalah music, you hear and feel the two distinct moods in the music.

The two moods together express the Kabbalist's relationship to and unification with the Creator. Even though the melody may bring one to tears, one loves to hear it because the melody expresses distress that has been dealt with and has been resolved in a good way. In Kabbalah, it is called "sweetening of judgments."

The music bathes the listener in a wondrous Light. We do not need to know anything about it before listening to it because it is wordless, yet its effect on our hearts is direct and swift. Hearing it over and over again is a special experience.

If you feel the music, you won't need to imagine the shapes in spiritual worlds, described in books. These shapes exist nowhere but within you and, therefore, mislead you. What is so special about the music is that everyone can understand it, even if we have not reached the composer's spiritual level. Listening to music composed by Kabbalists gives us all the opportunity to experience their spiritual sentiments.

MELODIES OF THE WORLD TO COME

The melodies in Kabbalah could be described as melodies of the "World to Come," as they serve the purpose of bringing the Upper Worlds to this world. Singing evokes blessings from Above so that they manifest in all lower worlds.

In the words of Rabbi Elazar Azikri (1533–1600), "Those who aspire shall sing praises unto spiritual heights, unto the Upper Ones and lower ones, fastening all the worlds with the tie of faith." (In Kabbalah, "faith" means attainment of the Creator.)

TUNING YOUR INNER INSTRUMENT

To understand what the Kabbalistic composer wants to express in the melody, you merely need to listen, and your understanding works automatically. By listening to the melodies of a Kabbalist, you have the opportunity to be affected to a certain degree by their impressions of the spiritual worlds.

There is a soul in each of us, and the soul of a Kabbalist resembles a musical instrument that plays properly and feels properly, similar to King David's biblical violin. This is no ordinary violin,

> **Spiritual Sparks**
>
> When a person acquires the quality of *Bina*, mercy, he or she feels calm and serene. Rav Baruch Ashlag expressed it in his gentle melody to the words from Psalms (116), "For thou hast delivered my soul."

but the inner *Kli* (vessel/instrument) of a Kabbalist's soul. In it, the Kabbalist feels reality in a certain way and can express it in melodies.

SPIRITUAL HARMONY

You can use Kabbalist tunes to connect to the spiritual roots from which they were written without having to work hard. Just relax and listen to the music.

Yet there is information in the notes themselves. The notes in Kabbalah are not random or "free form." Their harmony is built on Kabbalistic rules and notes are chosen according to the way a soul is built. They are a way to climb the ladder. You (the listener) feel them penetrating deep within your soul, unobstructed. This happens because of the direct connection between your soul and the roots of the notes.

Go back to Chapter 10 and think of the spiritual nature of Hebrew letters and their representation of numbers. The most important thing in Kabbalistic music is not the notes themselves, but all the fine nuances that exist between them.

Just to give you a sense of it, in Chapter 10 we said that there are *Taamim* (flavors), *Nekudot* (dots under, within, and above the letters), *Tagin* (tags on top of the letters), and *Otiot* (letters). These represent nuances formed by the impression from the Light—impressions, for instance, of *Reshimot* leaving and reentering the spiritual vessel.

It is the same with melodies. Musicians who understand how to play Kabbalistic melodies are few and far between. The difference between one who plays nicely and one who plays *correctly* lies in the extent to which one understands where the important things are. What's most important lies not in the sounds, but in the tiniest symbols, in how the sound begins and ends.

Spiritual Sparks

Singing is the call of the soul, ... the song, to which the Upper and the lower ones in all the worlds awaken. The song is like a spring from Above, a repose of the Upper One, the Divine mercy. The song adorns the Holy Supernal Name, *Malchut*, the receptacle of the Creator. And this is why it is the Holy of Holies.

—Rav Yehuda Ashlag

The Sulam Commentary on The Zohar

I had a wonderful student who played the violin. "I'm ready to play only on the condition that you will hold my hand," he would tell me. And he was right—Kabbalah music is about conveying the right feeling, not the accurate note.

IN A NUTSHELL

- Music is another medium for Kabbalists to express their spiritual states
- Kabbalah music lets you *feel* what the books express in text.
- Kabbalistic songs express the interplay of two moods: anguish over moving away from the Creator and joy over moving toward the Creator.
- In the end, all you need to do is relax, listen to the music, and try to be absorbed in the emotions the Kabbalists reveal in their music.

III

Kabbalah
Today

Y ou know what Kabbalah is and how it got started, but
how does it relate to today's world? In this section we'll
explore the reasons for the global crises we are facing

from the Kabbalistic point of view.

You may be asking, "What's in it for me?" Well, we'll also discuss your role in the big picture and how you can help heal yourself, your close environment, and the world at large.

Remember, we are all one soul. What happens to me affects you directly, so you have the ability to impact someone on the other side of the world. This final section will help you understand how to use Kabbalah to make the world a better place.

14

In the Global Era

JUST THE GIST
- How we affect each other
- United we stand, united we fall
- At the edge of the desire-sequence
- The potential (and danger) in great desires
- How selfish can we be

It is hardly news that the world is in a crisis. But the worst part is not that we don't feel as happy or safe today as we did yesterday; the worst part is the sensation that we have lost control. It seems more and more difficult to make our tomorrows brighter. And that's the real crisis.

A physicians' proverb says that an accurate diagnosis is half the cure; the entire healing process depends on it. In this chapter, we explore the roots of our crisis and the way to cure it. This chapter introduces the concepts, and the following chapters discuss in more detail the ideas presented here and their practical implementation.

OUR BIG BLUE MARBLE

When miners dig coal in China, the air in California gets polluted. When emissions from American cars dissolve in the air, the ice in Greenland melts. And when the ice in Greenland melts, the sea level rises and The Netherlands sinks.

It boils down to this: we are all part of the global village, and our actions affect one another.

THROUGH THICK AND THROUGH THIN

Of all the values you and I hold dear, the one we probably cherish most is privacy. We'd all like to have a piece of private property.

Back in Chapter 5, we said that there are five levels of desire: inanimate, vegetative, animate, human, and spiritual. We also said that there was once a single soul, called Adam, which broke into myriad fractions, which then dressed in physical bodies in our world. This is why we have so many people on planet Earth.

Spiritual Sparks

This entire reality, Upper and lower, is one ... and was emanated and created by a Single Thought. That Single Thought is the essence of all the operations, the purpose. It is, by itself, the entire perfection, the "One, Unique, and Unified."

—Rav Yehuda Ashlag, *The Study of the Ten Sefirot*

But no matter how far we feel from one another, we are still that one soul, Adam. If a brain cell is oblivious to a blood cell, it doesn't mean that it can live without it. Without the blood cells bringing food and oxygen to the brain, the brain cells would die—and so would the blood cells. So would we.

Through thick and through thin, united we stand and united we fall because united we are, already.

ASSUMING RESPONSIBILITY

Consider this: A newborn baby is responsible for nothing. How can it be? Because it cannot think about things and process them, because it cannot understand the world it experiences, a baby cannot be held responsible.

But an older child is already responsible for something, even if it's just to remember to put the sandwich in the lunchbox or to take the dog out at the end of a school day. A youth is already responsible for many more things, and a young adult is expected to take full responsibility for his or her life.

When we grow and have kids, we become responsible for others, too. But what if we were responsible for every single human being on Earth? What if that responsibility was not only to the people alive today, but also to all the people, animals, plants, and minerals that have ever lived since the moment of creation and to all eternity? This is the meaning of spiritual responsibility.

Now, this responsibility may sound like a heavy load, but what if that responsibility was not the result of some mean schoolteacher wishing to torment his students with an assignment they can't perform? What if it were simply the result of love?

We love our children, so responsibility for their well-being is not only natural, but welcome. What if we felt the same kind of love and care that we feel for our children toward the whole world and everything in it—toward all the creatures that ever lived, that are alive today, and that will be alive at any time in the future? That immense love is spiritual bliss. Kabbalah helps us experience this immense love, and make it inherent in our nature.

AS ONE UNIT

Remember how we started? First there was Adam, one soul. Adam was a good soul, wanting only to give to the Creator. But he misjudged his ability to give to the Creator, and that mistake cost him—and, consequently, us—heavily. He broke. His soul shattered into 600,000 pieces, which still today continue to break, hence the billions of people inhabiting our world. All of them are tiny fragments of the original soul.

The beauty of it is that each of us is both a particular soul and a piece in the puzzle of *Adam ha Rishon*. Within us are all the pieces of that first soul, just as every cell in our body contains all the genetic information to create a whole new identical body or a part of a hologram contains the entire image.

Tidbits

Here's the Kabbalistic explanation for the overpopulation on our planet. Our egoism keeps growing and becomes increasingly difficult to correct. The only way to correct it is by "splitting" it to tiny bits. For the egoism to correct, it needs to "dress" in a physical body. Thus, the number of people in the world is the number of fragments of the common soul (Adam) we currently need to correct.

But to realize that we are one soul, we have to want to feel this way. This simple rule runs throughout Kabbalah and spirituality: no coercion. In other words, you don't get what you don't want to get.

The cells in our bodies don't "think" about how they work together. They just function as one unit. We wouldn't make it past the first week of pregnancy if it hadn't been this way. Indeed, biology provides a perfect model for what Kabbalah describes as the common soul.

When a baby grows in its mother's womb, the minute cells begin to differentiate, a beautiful thing happens—they begin to communicate and cooperate with one another. The more differentiated they become, the more they are forced to cooperate. A liver cell can't do what a kidney cell does, so the kidney cleans up the toxins that the liver can't, and the liver creates the new cells that the kidney can't. This way, they are different but cooperating, and every part of the body benefits as a result.

THE TIME OF TOGETHERNESS

Just like our bodies, our souls can work cooperatively. We can live as separate units, just as there are unicellular creatures, but we all know that unicellular creatures are at the low end of nature's pyramid. The creatures at the top of the pyramid are multicellular creatures. Each cell in their bodies performs only one function, and all the cells collaborate to sustain the organism.

Kabbalists of the past attained spirituality on their own because they were unique souls with unique tasks, hence the fantastic nature of their achievements. But it's different today. Now that Kabbalah is open to all and studied by many, it's a safe bet that most of us will attain nothing individually. As a unit, however, we can achieve far more than has ever been achieved before.

For this reason, contemporary Kabbalists stress the importance of dispersing the knowledge of Kabbalah. They want the world to know so that more "cells" will join in the collective work of the soul, the spiritual body.

LITTLE ME IN YOU
LITTLE YOU IN ME

There are many offshoots to the fact that we are made of one shattered soul. One of them is that if I correct myself, I also correct my part in you. And vice versa. If you correct yourself, you also correct your "you" in me.

To bring it all down to earth, let's take three separate people as an example: Jack, James, and Mary. One day, Jack begins to feel his point in the heart and begins to correct himself. Jack has a little piece of James and a little piece of Mary within him, and the two others also have little pieces of the others in them. They are "cells" in the same spiritual body, and each cell contains all the genetic information to create a whole body.

When Jack corrects himself, the Jack in James and the Jack in Mary are corrected, too. Of course, the other two don't feel it because they're not Jack. Subconsciously, however, the Jack within them begins to urge the other two to start checking out this new concept of spirituality.

In this way, Jack subconsciously *inspires* them to check it out for themselves. His transformation serves as a model for theirs. This is because the basic structure of every human being is the same. We all have points in the heart, so we don't need to receive them from anyone. We need to merely listen openly and our own point in the heart will open. We've already talked in Chapters 3 and 7 about the importance of the social influence in determining the direction of our growth. If we want to become rich, we have to surround ourselves with people who want money. If we want to become lawyers, we surround ourselves with judges and advocates, and listen to what they say.

Off Course

If we are in an environment of people with a negative approach—to society or to themselves—we will inevitably begin to think like them. The way to make sure we progress in a positive direction is to surround ourselves with people who are on that direction, too.

We learn more than just techniques by talking to people we want to resemble. We absorb their *spirit*. Absorbing the spirit is the most important thing in everything we do, and it's the whole difference between success and mediocrity, or even failure.

The same goes with becoming spiritual. The best way to do it is to surround yourself with people who want spirituality. We all have more egoistic desires within us than anything else, and just one tiny speck of spirituality (true altruism)—a point in the heart.

So if many others talk to me about spirituality, I get inspired and think that everyone but me has loads of spirituality. Of course, it isn't true, but it does have the effect of making me want spirituality much more strongly, thus accelerating my progress. In turn, my progress accelerates others' progress, too, and their bogus spirituality becomes a reality.

SAVING OURSELVES ... AND EVERYTHING ELSE

Today many already realize that man is the only destructive element in nature. The reason for it is that we are not really part of nature. Our bodies belong to the animal kingdom, but our minds don't. Our minds are the reflection of our higher, spiritual self, which is still hidden from us.

Animals don't need to be taught how to behave because their behavior is hard-coded in them, written in their genes before they are born. If we were made of only the animal part in us, we'd be the same. But we're not, and therein lies the problem.

When babies learn to crawl, we must watch so they don't hurt themselves because their bodies can do things that their minds cannot monitor. For the children to avoid trouble, they don't need to develop their bodies further; they need to develop their minds so their minds will know what to do with their bodies.

There is a rule in Kabbalah: "General and particular are equal." It means that what is true for an individual is true for the whole, and vice versa. Just like a single baby, the whole of humanity must develop its mind so that its body—the collective body of humanity—will not harm itself.

Regrettably, we are slow learners. And this is why we are harming every creature and place on Earth, extinguishing its life and exploiting its minerals. In the process, we're also harming ourselves, probably more than we're harming any other creature. Just look at the rate of degenerative diseases today, and you'll see what we're doing to ourselves.

To stop this exploitation, we first have to correct our minds, and our minds can be corrected only if we correct the spiritual element in all of us.

SPIRIT OVER MATTER

In Kabbalah, the most basic rule is called "The higher degree rules." Spirit is Above matter. There is probably no dispute about that. So to change our world, we have to go to the place that corrupts it, and that place is the human mind.

As long as humans were only sophisticated animals, the world was fine. It was not in danger. But when we began to want to control it, when we started developing our egoism, that's when the troubles started, not just for ourselves, but for the world at large.

Spiritual Sparks

A will in the Upper One is a mandatory law in the lower one.

—Rav Yehuda Ashlag, *The Study of the Ten Sefirot*

If we correct our spirits, our bodies will act naturally, in harmony with the whole of nature, and hence with the Creator. Then we won't have to worry about saving virtually extinct animals. Nature will do it. After all, it had been doing it for millions of years before we came, and far better than we have ever succeeded.

ON THE DESIRE-SEQUENCE

There is a rule in Kabbalah: "He who is greater than his friend, his desire is greater than him." It means that if Jack, for instance, has a greater desire than James, Jack's desire is greater than Jack himself. In other words, in the correction process, we're always one step behind our own desires.

This is a deliberate process. It isn't that our desires grow. They only appear one by one, from lighter to heavier. When I finish correcting one desire, the next desire in line appears.

Remember the *Reshimot?* They form the desire-sequence that leads up the spiritual ladder. This is why Jack, who corrected his previous desire, is greater than James, who hasn't corrected this level of desire. But Jack's desire is greater than Jack himself because it is leading him to the next degree. More on that in just a bit.

DESIRES RUNNING RAMPANT

We've already said that desires grow from generation to generation. Our generation has the worst and strongest desire in the history of humankind. Kabbalists graphically demonstrate what they think of this generation with the words, "The face of the generation is as the face of a dog." Desire is running rampant to the point that people simply cannot find satisfaction anywhere—hence the soaring depression and violence rates in today's society.

But people in this generation aren't merely greedier than their parents were. Today, for the first time, there is a desire to know how things really work, to control Creation—to equalize with the Creator! This is a desire of millions of people, too, not just of a select few. More people are not settling for the answers provided by traditional means. They want to find out for themselves, and find out for certain. Taking someone else's word for it just doesn't do it for them any longer. These people need a method to reveal the overall design, and that method is Kabbalah.

TECHNOLOGY BROKE ITS PROMISE

As long as we are not using the method that can satisfy our deepest desire, to know the designer of the world and to learn from Him why He did it and how, we will not be happy. But as we've said before, the more we want, the more we develop our brains to provide us what we want.

Technology isn't going to stop just because we have a new desire. But as long as our technology is not accompanied by th study of the Upper Worlds, it will only make us feel worse.

isn't anything wrong with technology itself. It's just that it has become imbued with hopes that don't belong there. We think it can make us happier by making our lives faster, easier, more exciting. But all it can really do is show us more easily and more quickly that we are empty inside.

For knowledge to make us happy, it needs to be used for spiritual purposes. When we do that, what we know will open up new sides of itself that will make us see our world in a light we never dreamed existed. *The Upper World isn't a different place; it's a different perspective.*

A GREAT POTENTIAL

In light of what we've just said about growing desires and scientific progress, we can now begin to see our current situation from a spiritual point of view. In the past, people were not as mean and egoistic as they are today.

The gradual emergence of the *Reshimot* accounts for the change. When *Reshimot* of smaller desires appear, they don't seem like such mean desires. Today, however, the last and most egoistic *Reshimot* are appearing.

But this is not a bad thing. It's a lever for greater achievements. If we play our cards right—if we funnel these ferocious desires into the only constructive direction there is, the sky (or shall we say, heaven) is the limit.

WISHING FOR THE KING'S DAUGHTER'S HAND

We can't control which desires surface, but we can control what we do with them once they do. People still want money, power, and knowledge. But people are also getting frustrated and depressed because underneath the surface, the foundation of all those desires is spiritual. People want to control *everything*, they want to know *everything*.

Granted, most of us don't feel those desires. But we have them nonetheless because it's human nature to want *everything*. The only reason that we don't feel them is that we're realistic enough to know we will never have them, so we subconsciously prohibit them from surfacing.

In Kabbalistic terms, this is called "A man does not wish for the King's daughter's hand." Even so, knowing that I can't have the king's daughter doesn't mean that deep down I wouldn't like to. Thus frustration arises.

But the truth is that even if I did have the king's daughter, I wouldn't be satisfied. A desire that great really stems from the spiritual. It can be completely satisfied only through spiritual means.

If we direct these desires toward the root from which every desire and every pleasure comes, then we will experience the satisfaction of these desires immediately after we experience the desire itself. It would be like a never-ending chain of desires and pleasures endlessly linked.

What would we do then? Delightfully ride the wave.

SELFISH TO THE CORE

We don't have to worry about the kind of desires that surface in us. Deep within, we are all potential criminals of the worst kind you can imagine. But that doesn't mean that we have to act on those desires. Most of us don't.

But if we acknowledge those parts of ourselves, if we can begin to realize that we're that selfish, that's a very good start. We can then really start a change in ourselves and in the world around us.

No good thing ever came out of another good thing. Good things always grow out of crises because crises are opportunities for change. It is simple mathematics to see that because the present crisis is the worst, the opportunity for growth and for progress is greater than ever.

HOW TO START THE CHANGE

Now we're left with just one question: "What do I need to do?" That's the beauty of Kabbalah. You don't need *to do* anything, you need *to think*. Every now and again, hook up with Kabbalah, read something about it, watch a lesson on the video, talk about it with friends. That's enough to begin the change.

Nature created us egoists, and nature will change us. But for the change to happen, we need to want it to happen. That's all we need to worry about—wanting to change.

IN A NUTSHELL

- We're all connected and we all effect each other, for better or for worse.
- It is time to grow up and assume responsibility.
- Because we are all interrelated like cells in a body, we can change the whole by changing the parts.
- The desire to know how the world works and to understand the unseen secrets is greater than ever.
- The opportunity for growth and change is greater in this time of crisis.

15

DIAGNOSIS IS HALF THE CURE

JUST THE GIST
- Where is there free choice and who can make it?
- Nature's basic makeup
- Reality as reflection of our desires
- Are luxuries necessary?

In the last chapter, we presented the ills of society. As we said in Chapter 14, to cure the crisis, we must first diagnose it. This is half the healing. With that in mind, in this chapter we start looking at what we can practically do to find the root of our problem, and how Kabbalah allows us to take personal and societal action. We also review what we said about our perception of reality and show how you can put that information to use. As you'll see, by recognizing the evil in society and, more important, the evil in yourself, you'll be on your way to making the world a better place.

UNDERSTANDING NATURE

As is now quite evident, our world is on the brink of a catastrophe of gargantuan proportions. To understand the origin of the crisis, let's analyze the rudiments of nature itself. We start with the nature of human nature, as viewed from the perspective of Kabbalah.

TO GIVE OR NOT TO GIVE

Of all nature, only human beings relate to others with malicious intentions. No other creature harms, degrades, or exploits other creatures, derives pleasure from the oppression of others, or enjoys another's affliction.

The egoistic use of human desires, with the intention to elevate oneself at the expense of others, leads to a precarious imbalance with the surrounding world. Human egoism is the only destructive force with the ability to destroy nature itself. The danger to the world will persist until we change our egoistic approach to society.

Egoism of a part leads to the death of the whole. Look at it from a biological point of view. If a cell in a living organism begins to relate egoistically to other cells, it becomes cancerous. Such a cell begins to consume surrounding cells, oblivious to them and to the needs of the whole organism. The cell divides and multiplies unrestrainedly and eventually extinguishes the entire body, including itself.

The same applies to human egoism with respect to nature. While developing for itself, detached from the rest of nature and not as an integral part of nature, human egoism leads everything to extinction, including itself.

Cells can exist, develop, and multiply only by interacting as a single whole. This altruistic interaction functions in every being, even in human bodies, save for the human mind. The Creator gave us the freedom of will to fully perceive the need for altruism and to keep this comprehensive law of nature voluntarily—or not to.

As is well recognized in the media, globalization has compelled us to see the world as an interdependent whole. It may sound trite to say we're all connected, but trite or not, it's true. It's also true that many of the world's ills have developed because of the interconnectedness of societies. So will the solutions. They will come about only through the coexistence of all parts of nature and while each part works to sustain the *entire* system.

It is evident that humankind's problem is to balance each person's excessive desires with nature, to become an integral part of it and to act as a single organism. In Kabbalistic terms, humankind's task is to become altruistic.

NATURE'S BEDROCK

Altruism is defined as care for the wellbeing of one's fellow person. Research of altruism reveals that not only does it exist in nature, it is the very basis for the existence of every living thing. A living organism is one that receives from its environment and gives to it.

Every organism comprises a combination of cells and organs that work together and complement each other in perfect harmony. In this process, the cells are obliged to concede, influence, and help one another. The law of cell and organ integration according to the altruistic principle of "one for all" operates in every living organism.

Kabbalearn

Succinctly speaking, Kabbalistic altruism means working to increase the connectedness, the ties among the parts of the world.

Conversely, different natural elements, such as plants and animals, consist of different measures of a desire to be filled with power, vitality, and delight. The intensity of this desire creates nature's various levels: inanimate, vegetative, animate, and human.

Don't forget that each of the four levels—inanimate, vegetative, animate, and human—exists within each element in nature. Even a rock has a human part to it, as do plants and animals. What determines their outward appearance is the dominant level in them. In humans, the dominant level should be the human level, and because it's the highest, it controls all other levels. So you can see what happens when this level is malfunctioning. In Kabbalah, the human level is that part in us that has free choice. If we can develop a part within us that is totally untouched by calculation of self-gratification, we will truly be free—from our egos.

 Tidbits

At the risk of oversimplifying matters we can say this: To correct the world we need only follow Kennedy's advice, but make it more inclusive—Ask not what nature can do for you; ask what you can do for nature.

By attaining nature's unity under the principle, "one for all," we begin to perceive the uniqueness of humanity and its place in the world. The peculiarity of humans, compared to the rest of nature, lies in the power and nature of human desires and in their continuous evolution.

Altruism is connectedness for a higher purpose than the individual element in the collective. Human desires are the motivating force that propels and develops civilization. The trick is to use Kabbalah as a way to turn the developing egoistic desires into altruistic desires.

WHAT YOU SEE
IS WHO YOU ARE

How do you use Kabbalah to turn egoism into altruism? From a Kabbalistic point of view, the first thing to do is to realize that the corruption and egoism you see in the world around you are reflections of yourself on the inside. Let's see how.

In Chapter 3, we discussed the nature of perception. We said that the five human senses cannot perceive everything and that

Kabbalah develops a sixth sense, or *Kli*, which is the intention to use the desire to receive in order to give to the Creator.

We also showed how the senses perceive not the thing itself, but a personal interpretation of the thing, according to our qualities. On that basis, we suggested that what you perceive is influenced, if not determined, by what you already know, and what you experience is on the inside, not on the outside.

So what you and I see outside, in society, is really a reflection of our internal states, not an external reality. You and I are the society in which we live. As we'll see in the next chapter, the best thing you can do about the maladies of the world is to change yourself.

Before we head in that direction, however, one last look at human desire is necessary to clarify how our evolving desire is not only part of the problem, but also the solution.

Off Course

Correction works *only* from the inside out. We shouldn't fall into the trap of thinking that by changing our social and ecological environment we will be making any real change. As long as we haven't corrected our egoism, the world cannot truly be a better place.

MORE FOR ME
AND LESS FOR YOU

Save for humans, all of nature consumes only what it needs for sustenance. Humans crave more food, more sex, and more physical comfort than they need for their sustenance. This state is especially true in desires that are uniquely human, in the (endless) pursuit of wealth, power, honor, fame, and knowledge.

Desires for things that are necessary for existence are not considered egoistic, but natural because they come as nature's commands. These desires are present in the inanimate, vegetative, and animate, as well as in humans. Only those human desires that exceed what is necessary for existence are egoistic.

In addition to the fact that human desires grow exponentially, they incorporate pleasure from degrading others or seeing others suffer. These desires are unique to the human nature, and they are the real egoism. We experience them through our connections with others, and this is why the only way to correct our desires is to work on them with other people, as discussed in Chapter 11.

Spiritual Sparks

If we were not all so interested in ourselves, life would be so uninteresting that none of us would be able to endure it.

—Arthur Schopenhauer

(1788–1860), German philosopher

Our continuing indulgence in those desires indicates that we have not completed our evolution. But all desires can be considered altruistic or egoistic, depending on the purpose with which we use them. It turns out that the development of desires yields progress as well as crisis.

THE NECESSITY OF LUXURIES

Open your refrigerator and see what's in there. You'll find food from dozens of countries. And what those countries produce comes to them from dozens of other countries. Look at your clothes, your shoes—they come from all over the world, too.

Do you have to have it all?

The answer is twofold: we don't have to have it all if all we want is to survive. But if we want to have a life that we can call "life," the answer is most definitely "Yes." Moreover, we cannot control the evolution of our desires because they're determined by the *Reshimot*. That means that those of us who already want more than needed to merely survive cannot suppress their desires. Even if we try and succeed for a while, those desires will resurface and probably in a much more unruly manner.

For most of us, having all that we have in our refrigerators, closets, and garages *is a must*, not a luxury. This will be even more so in the coming years because our desires keep growing. Actually, if you think about the purpose of creation—and remember that the final goal is to acquire the Creator's mind—then what we want right now seems quite small in comparison.

The bottom line is that our will to receive is too great today for us to settle for providing for our sustenance. We want much more than that. We want cars and planes, we want to see the world. We want to vacation in resorts, we want to watch TV. So we don't have a choice. The only way to have great pleasures is to have great desires for them.

Now let's ask another question: What's wrong with wanting all that? Whom am I hurting by wanting to go to Hawaii for a luxury vacation? The answer is that the one who is hurt most by my desires is me. It's not that my desires are evil, it's that they don't give me true and lasting pleasure. And when they end, I am left twice as empty as before.

The recognition of evil we first mentioned in Chapter 3 is really the recognition that something *is bad for me*. What is not bad for me, I will never define it as evil. After all, every one of us is born completely self-centered and can therefore define something as bad *only* if it is bad for oneself.

So having great desires isn't bad in and of itself. What's bad is that when we satisfy them, we don't feel happy and fulfilled.

Spiritual Sparks

Man's heart is evil from his youth.

—Genesis, 8:21

But don't worry, for there is a good reason for all our desires and wants. These desires exist within us whether we are aware of them or not. But their root is much deeper and higher than, say, the beaches of Hawaii, as beautiful as those beaches may be.

WHY "DISGUISED" DESIRES FAIL US

Our desires for material things are rooted in the desire to receive pleasure, installed in us by the Creator back in Phase 1 (as described in Chapter 7): the pleasure of knowing the Creator, of being like Him. This desire is concealed by the chain of *Reshimot* as we climb down the spiritual worlds.

Today we are already climbing up the ladder, re-exposing the *Reshimot* of our desires even if we're unaware of it. Our decline has brought us to a state of complete detachment from the Creator, and in that sense, our egoism has fulfilled its role. In a world were the Creator is not tangibly sensed, we can freely choose between spirituality and corporeality, without any temptations to choose one way or another, except our own experience.

We explained in Chapter 7 that *Reshimot* are the soul's unconscious recollections of its past states. Now that we have come to the end of our decline, they are resurfacing in us, and we are experiencing intensifying desires for both material things and for more spiritual fulfillment (hence the spirituality and New Age trends, especially in the developed countries). Because these desires are actually cravings to experience the Creator, "disguised" as desires for other things (sex, wealth, power, etc.), when we provide them those other things, we don't experience fulfillment.

The trick—and here's where Kabbalah comes to our aid—is to keep our minds focused on the ultimate goal: the Creator. Desires come and go. But keeping our minds focused on the Creator prevents us from feeling disillusion when the satisfaction of a "disguised" desire fails to fulfill us.

If you work with this in mind, questions such as bad desires or good desires, luxuries and necessities, won't trouble you. Instead, you'll be bothered with much higher issues concerning your relationship with the Creator. This is why Kabbalists say that this world doesn't matter. Fulfillment exists only in spirituality, in your contact with the Creator.

In a sense, "bad" desires are actually good because they show us we haven't completed our work and where we still need to focus our attention on the Creator. When a desire first appears, you don't know that it's a desire for the Creator. You experience it as a desire for something in this world. Only when you strive to focus your attention on the Creator, despite your mundane thoughts, does the true nature of your desire (*Reshimo*) appears. At that point, you will discover that the desire was actually another facet of your desire for the Creator. This is how spiritual work happens on a day to day basis.

A HARMONIOUS PYRAMID

If we continue to focus on the Creator, and not on our own desires, we will eventually discover Him, by becoming like Him. When we become like Him, we discover that the whole of Nature is already like Him, existing in constant giving. Each level gives to the next, and the whole world lives in a harmonious pyramid.

SPIRITUALITY: A UNIQUELY HUMAN DESIRE

As we explained in Chapter 14, it's the law of nature that the highest degree rules over the lower degrees. Plants are higher than rocks, for instance, and you could make a case that plants help break down rocks over time for their own nourishment.

Animals rule over the plant world, and, in turn, humans rule over animals. In a sense, animals live at the expense of the inanimate and the vegetative, just as the vegetative lives at the expense of the inanimate. Each feeds on its lower degrees, but for a higher need than itself.

The higher orders have greater desires and, therefore, power over the lower degrees. Why?

A creature with a less-developed desire is like a baby. When the baby grows, it wants more things because its desire has evolved and can now detect more objects that are desirable. When it becomes an adult, the child becomes a man or a woman, goes to school, attends college, works and makes money, and has a career and family. One rises according to one's desire.

Kabbalearn

An animal feels life much more than a plant. It is alive, it breathes, it moves, and it has all kinds of sensitivities. It recognizes its habitat, its offspring, and its family, its pack. So the greater a creature is, the more it senses its existence, its selfness. That makes it greater and unique.

When desires push us, we become restless and progress. We don't have a choice. So desire is the motivating force for progress, for achievements.

Yet the egoistic desire drives us only to a certain point, until we despair of ever being satisfied and fulfilled this way. This is the journey we described at the beginning, in Chapters 1 and 2. This unsatisfied state forces us to change the method because we all ultimately want fulfillment. In that state, we begin to want spirituality, a uniquely human desire.

The will to receive grows even more. Gradually, as we learn about spirituality, we understand that fulfillment doesn't come only from benefitting ourselves directly, but from benefitting others. And *that* gives us the *real* fulfillment, just as a mother is happiest when her child is happy.

In short, the only way to have great pleasures is to have great desires. Great (unfulfilled) desires lead to emptiness. This, in turn, leads to the recognition of evil—that our desires are bad for us. Recognition of evil can lead to a desire for something entirely different, on a higher level. That something more is people's unique ability to desire and know the Creator.

THE POINT OF THIS WORLD

How does this desire to be similar to the Creator influence the rest of nature? We never influence anything at the level of this world. In this world, we can come to some decisions only according to what is in us and what we see. There are no actions in our world. Everything we do in our world is only to finally ask, "What is the point of all that?"

There is an animal level in us that wants a home, a family, and everything the body needs. There is a human level in us that wants money, honor, and knowledge. And there is Adam in us, the point in the heart that has a drive to be like the Creator. And this is the point of all that.

Precisely when one has a drive to be like the Creator, one changes. All other degrees can't change themselves in any way. They can't do anything. They simply exist the way they do. Only beings with a point in the heart have free choice. The free choice appears in the point in the heart. When the free choice appears, if we use it correctly, we become similar to the Creator.

This is really the only choice we have: to be or not to be similar to the Creator. Because only humans have points in the heart, only humans can have free choice, and only humans can change.

Correction begins when a person realizes that his or her egoistic nature is both a source of evil and the engine of change. It is a very personal and powerful experience, but it invariably brings one to want to change, to move toward altruism and away from egoism.

IN A NUTSHELL

- Humans are the only creatures with the choice to give or not to give.
- If we can develop the part within us that is totally untouched by calculation of self-gratification we will truly be free—from our egos.
- Reality reflects who we are. When it seems corrupt, it's because we are corrupt.
- The purpose of the existence of this world is to bring us to ask, "What's it all for?"

16

Correction Starts with Me

JUST THE GIST

- How He built the perfect world for correction
- What correction depends on (hint: it has to do with bonding)
- Why complete correction requires complete corruption
- The long and short ways to correction

It's easy to look at the world's problems and say, "There's nothing I can do ...." There *is* something you and I can do.

Up to this point, we have been learning the basics of Kabbalah and that the ego, or egoism, is our problem. The last two chapters focus on the way to correct our egoism. Naturally, to succeed in correcting the world, we have to first correct ourselves, which is the topic of this chapter.

DISCOVERING
THE UNIFIED STRUCTURE

As we've said throughout this book, Kabbalah provides a method by which you see that what happens inside you is how you experience the world outside you. We have also pointed out the interconnectedness of everything in creation. Tying these two is the key to correction.

At the end of the day, the wisdom of Kabbalah is very simple: there is an infinite desire to give, which created an infinite desire to receive. Because the desire to receive is infinite, it wants to receive its own Creator. The whole "story" of creation describes our attempts to realize that this is really how things are. As long as we feel separated from others, we have to work on how to experience this unified structure of desires. But when we are corrected, we will know that we are all one creation, and then correcting ourselves and correcting society are one and the same. So let's start breaking down the correction process into pieces we can work with.

LIVING IN A CREATORLESS BOAT

What you do affects the whole, and vice versa. A Kabbalah story from Rabbi Shimon Bar Yochai perfectly brings home the point. One of two people in a boat suddenly began to drill a hole in the bottom. His friend asked, "Why are you drilling?" The person drilling replied, "What business is it of yours? I am drilling under me, not under you."

Because all humankind is connected into one system, the irresponsible egoists subject themselves and all the others to suffering. It is the transformation activated by Kabbalah that makes us see the irresponsible egoists in ourselves and transform them into responsible adults, altruists in Kabbalistic terms.

Think back to Chapter 3 and remember that the Creator created only one soul, *Adam ha Rishon*. Then, in Chapter 8, we learned that he fell and his soul split into 600,000 parts. We've been trying to put them back together ever since. But for Adam to become equal to the Creator, he has to do something that will make him equal to the Creator. He must engage in giving.

Adam (you and I) is in a bind. If he gives because the Creator compels him to, it is not considered that *he* is giving, but that the Creator is forcing him to do it. To bring Adam to a state where he wants to give because the quality of giving is, in itself, of the highest value, without any thought of himself, the Creator must be concealed.

We have to feel as though we live in a "Creatorless" world, without guard and government from Above. We have to feel as though we alone make all the decisions and draw all the conclusions, including the conclusion that the quality of giving is the most worthy quality in reality. We are given the concealment of the Creator and the sensation that we are in contact with other people. Because the Creator (quality of giving) is hidden, we are egoistic and hate them, and they hate us. But at the same time, we are dependent on them, and they are dependent on us. This is precisely what globalization has been showing us so clearly in recent years.

So how do we reconcile our attitude toward society, where on one hand we need others and on the other we hate them and want to exploit them?

The Creator has put us between two forces, and we have a chance to see how we will choose. We can freely build ourselves as someone who gives to society, Above our nature, and without any consideration of ourselves, or we can choose to remain as egoistic as we are today.

Spiritual Sparks

When man is converted to loving others, he is in direct adhesion, which is equivalence of form with the Maker, and along with it man passes from his narrow world, full of pain and impediments, to an eternal world of bestowal to the Lord and to the people.

—Baal HaSulam,
"The Essence of Religion and Its Purpose"

By choosing to give above self-interest we make ourselves similar to the Creator. To the extent that we do it, the Creator opens up to us. He doesn't have to be hidden anymore because we have become like Him.

SALVATION IN BONDING OF EGOISTS

By the way, this explains why Adam fell. We had to first be created as a single creature and then be separated into egoistic, distanced, and detached individuals because this is the only way for us to see our complete oppositeness from the Creator.

There are many, many others like us around. The one soul of Adam divided into a multitude of souls (or bodies) to give each of us a chance to determine his or her attitude and choose whether he or she wants to be similar to the Creator.

The original soul was very pure when the Creator created it, with very small desires. But to receive all the pleasures that the Creator wants to give, a person must have an exaggerated, infinite desire to receive. The original soul had it, but unconsciously. These desires had to be made conscious and felt.

In addition, the creature had to feel that these desires are egoistic, which required that the creature be broken or divided, for a number of reasons.

First, it is impossible to correct a powerful will to receive if there is only one person. The Creator split Adam so that each person could correct the little egoism within. Even more, Adam split to have other people with whom to work. You and I need to bond with other egoistic people just like us in order to become similar to the Creator.

Finally, in a state of depravity, we can acknowledge the pettiness, limited nature, and hopelessness of our egoistic nature. We may then develop a desire to unite in order to transform our nature into the opposite, altruistic nature.

Now that you know the Kabbalistic explanation of Adam's story, what do you do? Others are treating you the way you are treating them because they are reflections of your attitude to the world. Because we try to exploit the world and treat it badly, we think that that's the way the world is treating us. The "scenario" of reality in our brain is negative, so reality seems negative to us. This naturally makes our world seem threatening and unsafe.

In that state, the only way to restore security and confidence is to unanimously agree to correct our egoistic desires. This is why we are discovering that simply to exist, we need each other. Moreover, we need to be treated well by everyone or we will not be able to escape the threat of destruction.

When we realize that we have no choice but to treat each other well, we will decide that we *have* to love our fellow beings and we will ask for this power from Above. This power will come from the Creator, from the Upper Light, and we will reach correction. Therein lies the inherent optimism of Kabbalah.

On Course

Kabbalah's statement that we are one interconnected soul isn't a philosophical statement; it places the responsibility for correction squarely in our laps. There is no correction to the world and to ourselves—on any level—without our active participation in mind, heart, and action.

A CHAIN OF SOULS

So we're all sharing life, just like cells in a body, where each cell depends on the life of the whole organism. If the other souls think about you, you will live. If they don't think about you, you will die. That law is the condition for spiritual, as well as physical life.

Today we are considered spiritually dead; the souls we have today are called "animate souls." The animate soul refers to our lives in this world, in a state of detachment from the Creator. Everything we feel and experience in this life, as long as we don't acquire a screen and develop the first spiritual *Kli*, is considered part of the animate soul. It exists for as long as we exist in this world, and disappears when we die. But these are far from the soul that Kabbalists refer to when they write about souls in *The Zohar* and other books. To have such a soul, we have to first decide that we want our soul, that we want eternal life, and that we want to be like the Creator.

Rav Yehuda Ashlag writes that all people throughout history are actually one long chain of souls. To see and experience this oneness of humanity, you must have an eternal soul that is connected to the eternal, to the Creator. That's the kind of soul that Kabbalists are talking about.

Now you see why your personal correction is so tightly connected to everybody else's correction. All souls are linked as one.

But here it's our own responsibility to choose. We have to decide that we want our souls, and we have to build our souls by ourselves, along with other souls.

In the language of Kabbalah, we say that souls are connected and integrated in a single body. For each soul to provide all the souls with what they need, all souls have to understand one another and realize that they are integrated in the others' desires. In other words, in your soul, you have to be incorporated with all the other desires, of all people, so you can provide them with what they want. Each cell in the body does just that; it feels what the body requires of it.

On a personal level, you must know what others need from you and provide what they need. In this way, you become like a complete body. You contain the

Off Course

In Kabbalah, there is a difference between what people *want* and what they *need*. What they want is what their egos tell them they want. What they need is a desire for spirituality because this is a desire for giving, the only lasting desire that can be fulfilled endlessly. By having a desire for spirituality, you feel eternal satisfaction because you sense both the desire and its satisfaction simultaneously.

Desire of others within you because of your love for them, and *you* want what *they* need.

When you work with others in that way, you feel that you, personally, have grown tremendously. Then you can give them what they need, and you become one unique and unified great creature, standing opposite the Creator.

THROUGH *HIS* EYES

When you want to give others what they need, you have become like the Creator. When you give someone else what he or she needs, you instill a part of yourself in the other person. As the other person receives, it begins to build in the other the understanding that giving to others is good, valuable, and—most importantly—pleasurable. In time, the giver begins to feel that it is not the giving to others that is pleasurable but the giving itself, the state of being a giver.

If you think about it for a moment, you'll see that nothing, even in our physical world, is created without giving. How can creatures be born without their parents' giving? Newborns are born because their parents love them and want to give to them, even before they come into existence.

This brings home one point: if this world exists, it means that its Creator loves it. If we, too, want to love our world, we have to learn to see it through His eyes, beyond our self-centered egos. If you want to give people what they need, you begin to see the world through the Creator's eyes, and thus, gradually, achieve the purpose of creation: acquiring the Creator's mind.

When you give because giving has merit in your eyes, without any direct or indirect benefits from the giving, it's considered that your actions are of your own free will. The giving is not for yourself, but for the sake of giving.

Of course, no act goes unrewarded because, as we've just explained, the Creator *wants* to give to us. But the reward for liking to give is seemingly detached from the giving itself. It's the revelation of the giver, the Creator. In other words, the reward for acting like the Creator is discovering the Creator and why He does what He does. By that you achieve the final correction, and the purpose of your creation.

Off Course

Love thy friend, or neighbor, as thyself, taught by the great Kabbalist Rabbi Akiva, is a maxim that virtually all religions and teachings have adopted. But this is a very dangerous maxim if lived without its final goal—reaching the Creator. Baal HaSulam writes that this is exactly what happened with Russia's communism. It was doomed to fail because it used nature's law of altruism without its final purpose: reaching the Creator through equivalence of form with Him.

The key to the whole process is a shift in thought and awareness. You need not change *anything* in the whole world except your *own* attitude to all the other souls, all the other people. This is why the saying "Love thy friend as thyself" is enough to correct the whole world. There is no other way to influence and change the world.

MY EGOISM IS MY OWN BANE

In the previous chapter we said that egoism is the engine of change. The greater your desires, the more evolved you are because when you want more, you can also receive more. You can achieve more because your will to receive drives you and gives you the strength to get what you want. Such a person is stronger because of his stronger willpower.

Because desires are egoistic by nature, they are initially ill-willed. In the end, that's bad for you, too. If you care only for yourself, you become detached from others and then can't fulfill yourself. The sensation of self-fulfillment depends on the existence of others. Thus, if I'm an egoist, I can't connect to others, and if I can't connect to others, I can't enjoy. My egoism has become my own bane. This leaves me poor, deficient and suffering. Because I have a big will to receive, I'm constantly chasing pleasures, yet I'm constantly empty.

This is the state that, as we have said, leads to a spiritual crisis. You realize that you can't go on living like that and understand that you have to change something in your life. Your point in the heart awakens, and in that state, all the evil in you can be turned into good.

ALL GROWN UP

As a result, the great desire leads to a choice that is, really, no choice. If we're so dependent on others, we have to care for them and watch over them, even if we hate them.

To survive and correct, we must tend to those we hate. If we don't, we will suffer.

So what should we do? Become true grownups. If we're that connected, we're also that responsible for one another. Just as grownups take responsibility for everything around them—their environment, their children, their employees, their friends, their cities and towns and countries. Everything and everyone. The Creator wouldn't want it any other way. It's His plan.

On Course

What greater pleasure is there for parents than to see their children grow up to become mature and successful adults? Similarly, the purpose for which the Creator created us is to be like Him. As a result, the goal of our lives in this world is to learn the Creator's ways of giving, learn His thoughts, and become like Him.

TWO WAYS UP

According to the Creator's plan, the entire universe must reach the state of correction, and the time allocated for correction is limited. *The Zohar* indicates that the correction must begin its final stages from the end of the 20th century. From this time on, humanity will be urged to correct by intensifying sufferings—read the news, and you'll see a fair case of that.

Recognizing the purpose of creation and knowing the method of correction will enable you to approach the goal consciously. This is the key, and it's faster than the suffering that will otherwise catch up with us from behind. Instead of suffering, we have the opportunity to feel fulfillment and inspiration even while still on the path of correction.

Remember from Chapter 7 how Kabbalah tells of a time frame for the final correction? The path to personal correction may take a while, but it will happen sooner or later. Plus, every soul must go through the process.

None of your experiences in life disappear. They are stored within your desire, and desires are eternal; they pass from one generation to another, from one incarnation to the next.

The next time you are born, as described in Chapter 11, your desire will retain the record of everything you did with regard to the Creator.

This is how the *Reshimot* play their role. Everything that you did inside your egoistical desire is stored in a "box," which eventually gives you the "recognition of evil." And until this box is filled completely, and until you correct all of your evil, you will continue to come to this world.

Next time you show up in this world, this "box" will contain what you have gained in your current round. The small steps you make accumulate and eventually yield results. Each step ultimately leads to spiritual elevation, but you get to experience the road as pleasurable and exciting or as painful and agonizing. You have a choice in the matter, and the last section in this chapter will explain how.

TAKE THE SHORT WAY, IT'S QUICK AND EASY

You can advance toward the realization that egoism is the root of evil through a long path of suffering or through a much shorter and delightful path of correction. Moreover, the path of suffering is not a path, merely the length of time needed for the realization that you need to march on the short path.

Yet as soon as a sufficient measure of suffering has been accumulated, you realize that there is greater profit in correction than in suffering, and you work to change. Instead of treading the long path, there is a short and easy path to correction.

Both paths are the same, but on the short path there are no phases of suffering, only constant progress. On the long path, however, there is suffering almost every step of the way.

The wisdom of Kabbalah is a tour guide to the short path. It tells you of all the states and helps you through them easily, with gentle encouragement.

You can acquire knowledge about the structure of the world, its causality and purpose *before* you are met with affliction. Through this knowledge, you accelerate the realization that egoism is bad and avoid the need to realize the evil in egoism under the threat of annihilation.

Although it seems that we are free to do as we please, in truth, we follow the commandments of our genes and adhere to the influence of the social environment. Those influences and commandments determine all our values, showing us how profitable it is to be powerful and prosperous.

We work hard all of our short lives only to win society's recognition of how successfully we keep its values. At the end of the day, we do not live for ourselves at all, but strain to find grace in the eyes of our children, our kin, our acquaintances, and society in general.

Clearly, succeeding in solving the crisis depends upon changing the values of society. That's the topic of the next chapter.

IN A NUTSHELL

- The Creator created a "Creatorless" boat, and we must keep it afloat.
- Only if we, egoists, unite we will survive.
- The Creator created the world with love. To be like the Creator means to love the world the way He loves it, to see it through His eyes.
- There are two ways to progress to spirituality: quickly and pleasantly, using Kabbalah, or slowly and painfully, without Kabbalah.

17

ALL TOGETHER NOW

JUST THE GIST
- How one little correction can make a huge difference
- The power of social values
- Where is Babel's broken tower?
- The benefits of true altruism

Kabbalah contains both personal and social aspects. As we discussed in the last chapter, we are all parts of the same collective soul. This chapter explains how the personal corrections presented in the last chapter flow through our connections to society. In the end, the individual correction we described in Chapter 16 is complete only when it contains a reciprocal connection with the entire humanity.

THE HEIGHT OF CREATION

Think back to Chapter 15, where we said that the source of all the suffering in the world is our oppositeness from the rest of nature. All other parts of nature—still, vegetative, and animate— follow nature's commandments instinctively and definitively.

Only human behavior places us in contrast to the still, vegetative, and animate practice.

Because humanity is the height of nature's creation, all other parts of nature depend on us. Through our correction, all parts of nature, the entire universe, will rise to its initial, perfect level, in complete unity with the Creator.

A DOMINO EFFECT

As we have said, the Creator treats all of us as a single, united being. We have tried to achieve our goals egoistically, but today we are discovering that our problems will be solved only collectively and altruistically.

The more conscious we become of our egoism, the more we will want to use the method of Kabbalah to change our nature to altruism. We did not do it when Kabbalah first appeared, but we can do it now because now we know we need it.

The past 5,000 years of human evolution have been a process of trying one method, examining the pleasures it provides, exhausting it, and leaving it for another. Methods came and went, and we have grown more prosperous, but not happier.

Now that the method of Kabbalah has appeared in force, aimed to correct the highest level of egoism, we no longer have to tread the path of disillusionment. We can simply correct our worst egoism through Kabbalah, and all other corrections will follow like a domino effect. During this correction, we can feel fulfillment, inspiration, and joy.

To review a little of the history presented in Chapters 5 and 6, The Book of Zohar states that starting from the end of the twentieth century, humanity will reach the maximum level of egoism and, at the same time, the maximum spiritual impoverishment in it. At that point, humanity will need a new method in order to survive.

Then, according to *The Zohar*, it will be possible to disclose Kabbalah, as the method of humanity's moral ascent to similarity with the Creator. This is why Kabbalah is revealed to humankind in these times.

Humanity is not corrected by everybody all at once. Rather, correction of humanity occurs to the extent that each person realizes his personal and general crisis, as covered in the last chapter.

Correction starts with a human being realizing that his or her egoistic nature is the source of all evil. Later, by changing the values of society, a person is subjected to society's influence.

The individual and one's social environment, the entirety of humanity, are bound by collective responsibility. In other words, humanity wanted to solve its problem egoistically and, hence, individually. Meanwhile, it found itself inevitably obliged to solve the problem collectively and, hence, altruistically.

In this respect, it is worth reflecting on Baal HaSulam's four factors that comprise us, which he explains in his essay, "The Freedom," and which we introduced in Chapter 3. To review and expand, the first factor is the source, the foundation, our inherent traits, which we cannot change because we inherit them from our parents. The second is how this source evolves, which we are also unable to change because it's determined by the source. The third factor is the environment, which we cannot change once we are in it.

The fourth factor, however, is the changes in the environment, and *those we can and must* change by choosing the environment that is right for us. The fourth factor affects the third, which affects the second, which affects the first. By building the right environment for our spiritual purposes, we build a society that not only changes us toward spirituality, but also makes everybody else's way to spirituality much easier and faster. Now let's see how we can put this theory into action.

LET'S AGREE ON GIVING

If everyone thinks giving is good, then I, too, will think giving is good, out of my own egoistic interest. This is so because altruistic behavior is profitable for all.

Altruism rules in education, for instance. Schools teach us to be altruists. We are told to be honest, hard-working, and respectful of others; to share with others what we have; to be friendly; and to love our neighbors. All this happens because altruism is beneficial to society.

Furthermore, the biological laws of living organisms teach us that the existence of an organism depends on the cooperative work of all its parts, as recounted in Chapters 15 and 16.

> **Spiritual Sparks**
>
> Anyone who is experienced knows that there is one issue in the world, which is the greatest of all imaginable pleasures, namely finding grace in the eyes of people, for which every effort is worthwhile.
>
> —Rav Yehuda Ashlag

Similarly, the perception of the benefits of altruistic behavior is present in an egoistic human society. No one actively opposes altruistic acts. On the contrary, every organization and public figure advertises his, her, or its involvement in altruistic actions and takes pride in them. No one overtly denounces the spreading of altruistic ideals.

THE POWER IN THE APPRECIATION OF SOCIETY

The means to change our behavior from egoistic to altruistic is to change our priorities and value hierarchy. We need to be convinced that bestowal to society is much more important and worthwhile than receiving from it. In other words, each person must come to feel much greater fulfillment from giving to society than from any egoistic acquisition.

Public opinion is the only means to facilitate this goal because the single most important thing for every person is the appreciation of society. Humans are built in such a way that receiving the sympathy of society is the purpose of life.

This element is so intrinsic that people tend to deny that the purpose of every action is to acquire society's appreciation. We might claim that we are motivated by curiosity or even money, but we would not admit to the real incentive: the recognition of society.

We are built in such a way that the human environment determines all our predilections and values. We are entirely and involuntarily controlled by public opinion. This is why society can infuse its members with any mode of behavior and any value, even the most abstract or absurd.

DENOUNCE EGOISM AND EXTOL ALTRUISM

Modifying society's tasks will require changing the education systems, starting from a very early age, as well as cardinal transformations in all areas of education and culture. All media will have to praise and evaluate events according to their benefit to society, thus creating an environment of education for bestowal upon society. Using every means of mass media, advertisement, persuasion, and education, the new public opinion should openly and resolutely denounce egoistic actions and extol altruistic actions as the ultimate value.

Through society's purposeful influence, everyone will aspire to receive only what is necessary for sustenance from society and spare no effort to benefit society, in order to receive society's appreciation. At first, everyone will work to benefit society under environmental encouragement and influence. People will feel satisfied, and we will begin to see the act of bestowal upon society as the ultimate unique value, even without reward from the environment for each act of giving.

It isn't just social institutions that need to change. So must the most prevalent and, in some ways, most "dug in" social institution: the family.

If my children at home look at me and appreciate me according to society's appreciation of me, and if my children appreciate me according to how much I give to society, then I am more likely to change.

If my kin and co-workers and generally everyone appreciate me only according to what I give to society, then I will not have a choice. I will have to contribute. I will have to become a net giver to all.

All this activity will raise the level of human consciousness to the level of a new civilization.

Off Course

We must be very careful here. Past attempts to use society and kin to altering social values have produced the most terrible atrocities, including the Nazis and Stalin's communism. This is *not* what Kabbalah refers to when it suggests that we use society to change our values. Kabbalah merely suggests that we encourage everyone that giving is profitable and pleasurable. Then, when more people believe it, I, too, will believe it, even if at first I was coaching others to believe it without believing it myself.

"Rabbi Ashlag was passionately committed to that far-reaching social vision, as it emerged from his understanding of the Kabbalistic tradition," writes Micha Odenheimer in *Latter-Day Luminary*: "He grasped humanity as a single entity, both physically and spiritually interdependent, and believed that only an economic system that recognized this could liberate humankind and catalyze an era of collective enlightenment."

By developing a community based on love among its members and a society founded on economic justice, Odenheimer writes, Kabbalah provides a focus on individual consciousness and the mending of society and the world. Rabbi Ashlag's contribution is a "concept of social justice founded on the spiritual science of Kabbalah."

UNDERSTANDING
BABEL'S TOWER

In ancient times, humans were not so egoistic as to be opposite to nature. They felt nature and their fellow persons reciprocally. This was their language of communication, which, for the most part, was a silent language, similar to telepathy, on a certain spiritual level.

Increased egoism, however, detached humans from nature. Instead of correcting the oppositeness, humans thought they would be able to attain the Creator egoistically, not through correction.

As a result, they stopped perceiving nature and their fellow humans, stopped loving, and started hating one another. This separated us from each other and instead of being one nation, we split into many.

The first level of egoistic development is marked by what we allegorically call "building of the Tower of Babel." In the story of Babel, you may recall, people, out of increased egoism, aspired to reach the Creator, allegorically described as wanting to build a tower whose head reaches the sky.

Humanity failed to direct its increased egoism toward the attainment of the governing forces because this method of attainment demanded of us to curb egoism, and we failed to do that.

People's increased egoism made them stop feeling each other and the spiritual connection; the telepathy was broken. Because they knew of the Creator from their previous level of egoism, they now wanted to exploit Him as well. That's what was meant by building a tower that reaches the sky. As a result of their egoism, they stopped understanding each other, and their oppositeness from nature alienated them from it and from the Creator, and they dispersed.

We may have compensated for it with technological development. But in doing so, we have only increased our detachment from one another and our alienation from nature (the Creator). So now humanity is becoming disillusioned with fulfilling the egoism solely by social or technological development.

We are realizing that egoistic desires cannot be filled in their natural form. The very fulfillment of a desire annuls it. As a result, the desire is no longer felt, just as food reduces the sensation of hunger and, along with it, the pleasure from eating is gradually extinguished.

Particularly today, as we acknowledge the crisis and the dead-end point of our development, it can be said that the confrontation of the egoism with the Creator is the actual destruction of the Tower of Babel.

Formerly, the Tower of Babel was ruined by the Upper Force. Today it is being ruined in our own consciousness. We are at a similar separation point that occurred in the time of Babel, except now we are aware of our situation. According to the wisdom of Kabbalah, the global crisis is the beginning of the reconnection of all humanity into a new and united civilization.

It is time for the members of the single nation of humankind to reunite into a united people. Spiritual fulfillment provides a path and a perhaps unexpected truth.

ENHANCED PERCEPTION

How much is one plus one? The answer is *Ein Sof* (infinity). Each of us is integrated with everybody else, and for this reason, with just one more person to work with, we can simulate a society. This, in turn, simulates our relationship with the Creator. The reward is huge.

Indeed, there is a special bonus to altruism. It may seem as if the only change will be putting others before ourselves, but there are actually far greater benefits. When we begin to think of others, we become integrated with them, and they with us.

Actually, each of us is *Ein Sof*, but without a society to help you correct yourself, how will you feel it? If you remember one of Kabbalah's basic rules that the whole and the part are the same, your life will be much easier. You will be able to work on the whole (society) knowing that you are actually working on yourself, and this will make your correction much easier.

Think of it this way: there are about 6.5 billion people in the world today. What if, instead of having two hands, two legs, and one brain to control them, you had 13 billion hands, 13 billion legs, and 6.5 billion brains to control them?

Confusing? Not really, because all those brains would function as a single brain, and the hands would function as a single pair of hands. All of humanity would function as one organism whose capabilities were enhanced 6.5 billion times. After all, there are much more than 6.5 billion cells in our body, but it still functions as one unit. So if a single body can do it, why not the whole of humanity?

In addition to becoming superhuman, anyone who became altruistic would receive the most desirable gift of all: omniscience, or total recall and total knowledge. Because altruism is the Creator's nature, acquiring it equalizes our nature with His, and we begin to think like Him. We begin to know why everything happens, when it should happen, and what to do if we want to make it happen differently. In Kabbalah, this state is called "equivalence of form," and attaining it is the purpose of creation.

BEYOND LIFE AND DEATH

This state of enhanced perception, of equivalence of form, is why we were created in the first place. This is why we were created united and were then broken—so we could reunite. In the process of uniting, we will learn why nature does what it does and will become as wise as the Thought that created nature.

When we unite with nature, we will feel as eternal and complete as nature. In that state, even when our bodies die, we will feel that we continue to exist in the eternal nature.

Physical life and death will no longer affect us because our previous self-centered perception will have been replaced with holistic, altruistic perception. Our own lives will have become the life of the whole of nature.

But if you've gotten this far, no matter what you might think, it's really even simpler than it sounds. You can already relate to Eternity. We're already in *Ein Sof*. We're just unaware of it. With the wisdom of Kabbalah, we have a great guide. With great guides, we can all find our way.

IN A NUTSHELL
- Humans are the height of creation, so when we are corrected, everything else will follow.
- The first thing to do is to agree that giving is good.
- The most powerful force, and the motivation behind our actions, is our desire for society's appreciation.
- To create a shift in society, there must be open denunciation of egoism and extolling of altruism.
- Babel's tower is broken in our minds, in our separation from each other. When we correct it, we will obtain not only love for each other, but the mind of the Creator, and existence beyond life and death.

Appendix

GLOSSARY

Abraham: A man born in Babylon who discovered the wisdom of Kabbalah, taught it to all who were interested, and started the first Kabbalah group, which later became the nation of Israel. *Sefer Yetzira* (*The Book of Creation*) is ascribed to him.

Adam: *See Adam ha Rishon.*

Adam ha Rishon: The Kabbalistic name of Adam, the original soul. The breaking of Adam's soul caused the division of Adam's soul into 600,000 particular souls or individual desires.

Altruism: Working for the gratification of the system of creation regardless of one's own desires.

Bestowal: The Creator's quality of giving without thinking of Himself. This is the quality the creatures (us) need to acquire in order to become like Him and discover Him.

Bina: Understanding. In Kabbalah, it generally refers to the contemplation of the ways of cause and effect and to benevolence. It also means the quality of giving, *Hassadim* (Mercy), which is the quality of the Creator.

Correction: Kabbalists refer to correction to mean turning the intention with which we use a desire from "for me" to "for the Creator." No one will tell you that you are correct or incorrect. But if you've used a desire to make you more "Creatorlike," you've done the correct thing.

Degree: *See* Spiritual Degree.

125 degrees: Between the Creator and creation there are five worlds, with five *Partzufim* in each world, and five *Sefirot* in each *Partzuf*. If you multiply 5 worlds × 5 *Partzufim* × 5 *Sefirot*, you get 125 degrees. *See also* spiritual degree, *Sefirot*.

Egoism: Working for self-gratification regardless of the needs of the system of creation.

Equivalence of Form: The form (quality) of the Creator is bestowal; the form of the creature is reception. When one can learn to receive with the intention to bestow, it is considered that one has equalized one's form with the Creator's: both are now givers.

Faith: The quality of bestowal; clear perception of the Creator.

Four Phases of Direct Light: The first five stages, root (0)–4, by which the Thought of Creation created *Malchut*, the will to receive, and the root of all creations.

Free choice: A choice made without being partial toward oneself. To have free choice, one has to be Above one's ego, in the spiritual world.

Haman: One of the names given to the will to receive.

Intention: The direction in which a desire is used—for you or for the Creator.

Kabbalah: A science that provides a detailed method of showing you how to perceive and experience the spiritual worlds, which exist beyond what you can perceive with your five senses. Kabbalah means "Reception" in Hebrew.

Kabbalists: People who have acquired additional senses because they have attained the ability to *lekabel* ("to receive" in Hebrew) higher knowledge. The method that enables people to transcend the boundaries of their nature is called *Kabbalah* ("reception" in Hebrew) because it enables them to know the true reality.

Kli: (vessel) The sixth sense; the will to receive with a *Masach* (screen) on it.

Law of Correction: States that first the easiest parts are corrected; and then, with their help, the tougher parts are handled.

Light: Pleasure, the force of bestowal that operates and fills the whole reality.

Masach (screen): The ability to reject the Creator's Light if it is not in order to give back to Him.

Mordechai: The will to bestow.

Moses: The greatest prophet and the next great Kabbalist after Abraham. Wrote the *Torah* (Pentateuch) and taught Kabbalah to all who listened. Moses is the point in the heart in everyone of us, the desire for spirituality.

Olam (World): There are five worlds between the Creator and creation—*Adam Kadmon*, *Atzilut*, *Beria*, *Yetzira*, and *Assiya*. The word *Olam* comes from the word *Haalama* (Concealment). The name of the *Olam* designates a specific measure of concealment of the Creator's Light from creation (us).

Partzuf (Face): A *Partzuf* is a complete structure of ten *Sefirot* with a *Masach* that can determine which *Sefira* receives Light and which doesn't.

Person (in this world) : Means that the will to receive is in a state of concealment from the Creator, with no intention to receive from Him or to give to Him.

Point in the heart: The last degree in the evolution of human desire, the desire for spirituality.

Prayer: Any desire is a prayer. But a prayer that is answered is a desire to be corrected, to becoming like the Creator. A prayer is called "the work in the heart."

Purpose of Creation: The reason the Creator created creation is for it to receive the ultimate pleasure: being like Him. This is the purpose of creation.

Rabbi Isaac Luria (the Holy Ari): A great Kabbalist who lived in the 16th century in Israel. Author of *The Tree of Life.*

Rabbi Shimon Bar-Yochai (Rashbi): Author of 2nd century CE *The Book of Zohar*, the seminal text of Kabbalah. Rashbi was the student and successor of Rabbi Akiva, the great Kabbalist who taught "Love thy friend as thyself."

Rav Yehuda Ashlag: The last great Kabbalist (1884–1954). Known as Baal HaSulam (owner of the ladder) for his *Sulam* (Ladder) commentary on *The Book of Zohar.*

Reality: The part of the Creator's Light that a person can perceive, depending on one's inner structure. Because of that, reality is always subjective.

Reincarnation: A reincarnation is every time you make a step in spiritual growth. If you correct yourself intensely, you can experience many lifetimes in a matter of minutes.

Reshimot: The soul's unconscious recollections of its past states.

Root of the Soul: The place of the soul in the system of *Adam ha Rishon.*

Sanctity: An exalted state in which you ascribe everything to the Creator. You realize that there is none else besides him and that you are equal to Him in your attributes.

Screen: *See Masach.*

Sefirot: The 10 basic qualities of the spiritual world. Their names are *Keter, Hochma, Bina, Hesed, Gevura, Tifferet, Netzah, Hod, Yesod,* and *Malchut.* Sometimes they are divided into five, and then you have *Keter, Hochma, Bina,* and *Zeir Anpin,* which includes the *Sefirot Hesed, Gevura, Tifferet, Netzah, Hod,* and *Yesod.* The last *Sefira* is *Malchut.*

Shame: *Malchut's* sensation of her oppositeness from the Creator. When *Malchut* realizes that she only receives and that He only gives (to her), she is so ashamed that she stops receiving, and makes the *Tzimtzum* (restriction).

Soul: A desire to receive with a *Masach* and the intention to bestow is called "a soul." Also, *Adam ha Rishon* is considered the common soul from which we all come. Adam represents the first person to have a *Masach,* and we are all his "spiritual" children. See also *Adam ha Rishon.*

Spiritual degree: An ability to receive a certain amount (and kind) of pleasure with the intention to bestow upon the Creator.

Surrounding Light: The Light that wishes to fill creation, as well as the Light that is destined to transform egotistical desire into altruistic one.

Tetragrammaton: In Greek, literally "four-letter word." Designates the sacred name of God. In Hebrew, it is the *HaVaYaH* (*Yod, Hey, Vav, Hey*), or the Four Phases of Direct Light.

The Book of Zohar: Written around 2nd century CE by Rabbi Shimon Bar-Yochai and his group. This is the seminal book of Kabbalah. It was hidden right after it was written and reappeared in the 13ᵗʰ century in possession of Rabbi Moshe de Leon. Probably for this reason, there are scholars who consider Moshe de Leon to be its author, although Moshe de Leon himself claimed that he did not write the book, but Rabbi Shimon Bar-Yochai.

Torah: Five Books of Moses. Torah means "Light" as well as "instruction." The text of the Torah holds within it the instructions to receive all the Light of the Creator, if you know how to read it right. Today, we need to study Kabbalah to be able to understand it correctly.

The Tree of Life: The Ari's (Rabbi Isaac Luria) principal text. This text is still at the heart of contemporary Kabbalah. Because of the importance of the Ari's book, the term *Tree of Life* has become a synonym of the term *The Wisdom of Kabbalah*.

Tzimtzum (Restriction): Not receiving Light despite wanting it. When *Malchut* discovers that she is opposite from the Creator, her shame makes her stop receiving His Light although she has a great desire for it.

World: *See Olam.*

Yam Suf: The Red Sea. *The Book of Zohar* calls the Red Sea "the Sea of the End," representing the ego's final frontier. Beyond *Yam Suf* begins the spiritual world.

FURTHER READING

To help you determine which book you would like to read next, we have divided the books into five categories—Beginners, Intermediate, Advanced, Good for All, and Textbooks. The first three categories are divided by the level of prior knowledge readers are required to have. The Beginners Category requires no prior knowledge. The Intermediate Category requires reading one or two beginners' books first; and the Advanced level requires one or two books of each of the previous categories. The fourth category, Good for All, includes books you can always enjoy, whether you are a complete novice or well versed in Kabbalah.

The fifth category—Textbooks—includes translations of authentic source materials from earlier Kabbalists, such as the Ari, Rav Yehuda Ashlag (Baal HaSulam) and his son and successor, Rav Baruch Ashlag (the Rabash).

Additional translated material that has not yet been published can be found at **www.kabbalah.info**. All materials on this site, including e-versions of published books, can be downloaded free of charge.

BEGINNERS

Kabbalah for Beginners

Kabbalah for Beginners is a book for all those seeking answers to life's essential questions. We all want to know why we are here, why there is pain, and how we can make life more enjoyable. The four parts of this book provide us with reliable answers to these questions, as well as clear explanations of the gist of Kabbalah and its practical implementations.

Part One discusses the discovery of the wisdom of Kabbalah, and how it was developed, and finally concealed until our time. Part Two introduces the gist of the wisdom of Kabbalah, using ten easy drawings to help us understand the structure of the spiritual worlds, and how they relate to our world. Part Three reveals Kabbalistic concepts that are largely unknown to the public, and Part Four elaborates on practical means you and I can take, to make our lives better and more enjoyable for us and for our children.

Kabbalah Revealed

This is the most clearly written, reader-friendly guide to making sense of the surrounding world. Each of its six chapters focuses on a different aspect of the wisdom of Kabbalah, illuminating its teachings and explaining them using various examples from our day-to-day lives.

The first three chapters in *Kabbalah Revealed* explain why the world is in a state of crisis, how our growing desires promote progress as well as alienation, and why the biggest deterrent to achieving positive change is rooted in our own spirits. Chapters Four through Six offer a prescription for positive change. In these chapters, we learn how we can use our spirits to build a personally peaceful life in harmony with all of Creation.

Wondrous Wisdom

This book offers an initial course on Kabbalah. Like all the books presented here, *Wondrous Wisdom* is based solely on authentic teachings passed down from Kabbalist teacher to student over thousands of years. At the heart of the book is a sequence of lessons revealing the nature of Kabbalah's wisdom and explaining how to attain it. For every person questioning "Who am I really?" and "Why am I on this planet?" this book is a must.

Awakening to Kabbalah

A distinctive, personal, and awe-filled introduction to an ancient wisdom tradition. In this book, Rav Laitman offers a deeper understanding of the fundamental teachings of Kabbalah, and how you can use its wisdom to clarify your relationship with others and the world around you.

Using language both scientific and poetic, he probes the most profound questions of spirituality and existence. This provocative, unique guide will inspire and invigorate you to see beyond the world as it is and the limitations of your everyday life, become closer to the Creator, and reach new depths of the soul.

Kabbalah, Science, and the Meaning of Life

Science explains the mechanisms that sustain life; Kabbalah explains why life exists. In *Kabbalah, Science, and the Meaning of Life*, Rav Laitman combines science and spirituality in a captivating dialogue that reveals life's meaning.

For thousands of years Kabbalists have been writing that the world is a single entity divided into separate beings. Today the cutting-edge science of quantum physics states a very similar idea: that at the most fundamental level of matter, we are all literally one.

Science proves that reality is affected by the observer who examines it; and so does Kabbalah. But Kabbalah makes an even bolder statement: even the Creator, the Maker of reality, is within the observer. In other words, God is inside of us; He doesn't exist anywhere else. When we pass away, so does He.

These earthshaking concepts and more are eloquently introduced so that even readers new to Kabbalah or science will easily understand them. Therefore, if you're just a little curious about why you are here, what life means, and what you can do to enjoy it more, this book is for you.

From Chaos to Harmony

Many researchers and scientists agree that the ego is the reason behind the perilous state our world is in today. Laitman's groundbreaking book not only demonstrates that egoism has been the basis for all suffering throughout human history, but also shows how we can turn our plight to pleasure.

The book contains a clear analysis of the human soul and its problems, and provides a "roadmap" of what we need to do to once again be happy. *From Chaos to Harmony* explains how we can rise to a new level of existence on personal, social, national, and international levels.

INTERMEDIATE

The Kabbalah Experience

The depth of the wisdom revealed in the questions and answers within this book will inspire readers to reflect and contemplate. This is not a book to race through, but rather one that should be read thoughtfully and carefully. With this approach, readers will begin to experience a growing sense of enlightenment while simply absorbing the answers to the questions every Kabbalah student asks along the way.

The Kabbalah Experience is a guide from the past to the future, revealing situations that all students of Kabbalah will experience at some point along their journeys. For those who cherish every moment in life, this book offers unparalleled insights into the timeless wisdom of Kabbalah.

The Path of Kabbalah

This unique book combines beginners' material with more advanced concepts and teachings. If you have read a book or two of Laitman's, you will find this book very easy to relate to.

While touching upon basic concepts such as perception of reality and Freedom of Choice, *The Path of Kabbalah* goes deeper and expands beyond the scope of beginners' books. The structure of the worlds, for example, is explained in greater detail here than in the "pure" beginners' books. Also described is the spiritual root of mundane matters such as the Hebrew calendar and the holidays.

ADVANCED

The Science of Kabbalah

Kabbalist and scientist Rav Michael Laitman, PhD, designed this book to introduce readers to the special language and terminology of the authentic wisdom of Kabbalah. Here, Rav Laitman reveals authentic Kabbalah in a manner both rational and mature. Readers are gradually led to understand the logical design of the Universe and the life that exists in it.

The Science of Kabbalah, a revolutionary work unmatched in its clarity, depth, and appeal to the intellect, will enable readers to approach the more technical works of Baal HaSulam (Rabbi Yehuda Ashlag), such as *The Study of the Ten Sefirot* and *The Book of Zohar*. Readers of this book will enjoy the satisfying answers to the riddles of life that only authentic Kabbalah provides. Travel through the pages and prepare for an astonishing journey into the Upper Worlds.

Introduction to the Book of Zohar

This volume, along with *The Science of Kabbalah*, is a required preparation for those who wish to understand the hidden message of *The Book of Zohar*. Among the many helpful topics dealt with in this text is an introduction to the "language of roots and branches," without which the stories in *The Zohar* are mere fable and legend. *Introduction to the Book of Zohar* will provide readers with the necessary tools to understand authentic Kabbalah as it was originally meant to be, as a means to attain the Upper Worlds.

The Book of Zohar:
annotations to the Ashlag commentary

The Book of Zohar (*The Book of Radiance*) is an ageless source of wisdom and the basis for all Kabbalistic literature. Since its appearance nearly 2,000 years ago, it has been the primary, and often only, source used by Kabbalists.

For centuries, Kabbalah was hidden from the public, which was deemed not yet ready to receive it. However, our generation has been designated by Kabbalists as the first generation that *is* ready to grasp the concepts in *The Zohar*. Now we can put these principles into practice in our lives.

Written in a unique and metaphorical language, *The Book of Zohar* enriches our understanding of reality and widens our worldview. Although the text deals with one subject only—how to relate to the Creator—it approaches it from different angles. This allows each of us to find the particular phrase or word that will carry us into the depths of this profound and timeless wisdom.

GOOD FOR ALL

Attaining the Worlds Beyond

From the introduction to *Attaining the Worlds Beyond*: "...Not feeling well on the Jewish New Year's Eve of September 1991, my teacher called me to his bedside and handed me his notebook, saying, 'Take it and learn from it.' The following morning, my teacher perished in my arms, leaving me and many of his other disciples without guidance in this world.

"He used to say, 'I want to teach you to turn to the Creator, rather than to me, because He is the only strength, the only Source of all that exists, the only one who can really help you, and He awaits your prayers for help. When you seek help in your search for freedom from the bondage of this world, help in elevating yourself above this world, help in finding the self, and help in determining your purpose in life, you must turn to the Creator, who sends you all those aspirations in order to compel you to turn to Him.'"

Attaining the Worlds Beyond holds within it the content of that notebook, as well as other inspiring texts. This book reaches out to all those seekers who want to find a logical, reliable way to understand the world's phenomena. This fascinating introduction to the wisdom of Kabbalah will enlighten the mind, invigorate the heart, and move readers to the depths of their souls.

Basic Concepts in Kabbalah

This is a book to help readers cultivate an approach to the concepts of Kabbalah, to spiritual objects, and to spiritual terms. By reading and re-reading in this book, one develops internal observations, senses, and approaches that did not previously exist within. These newly acquired observations are like sensors that "feel" the space around us that is hidden from our ordinary senses.

Hence, *Basic Concepts in Kabbalah* is intended to foster the contemplation of spiritual terms. Once we are integrated with these terms, we can begin to see, with our inner vision, the unveiling of the spiritual structure that surrounds us, almost as if a mist has been lifted.

Again, this book is not aimed at the study of facts. Instead, it is a book for those who wish to awaken the deepest and subtlest sensations they can possess.

Together Forever

On the surface, *Together Forever* is a children's story. But like all good children's stories, it transcends boundaries of age, culture, and upbringing.

In *Together Forever*, the author tells us that if we are patient and endure the trials we encounter along our life's path, we will become stronger, braver, and wiser. Instead of growing weaker, we will learn to create our own magic and our own wonders as only a magician can.

In this warm, tender tale, Michael Laitman shares with children and parents alike some of the gems and charms of the spiritual world. The wisdom of Kabbalah is filled with spellbinding stories. *The Magician* is yet another gift from this ageless source of wisdom, whose lessons make our lives richer, easier, and far more fulfilling.

TEXTBOOKS

Shamati

Rav Michael Laitman's words on the book: Among all the texts and notes that were used by my teacher, Rav Baruch Shalom Halevi Ashlag (the Rabash), there was one special notebook he always carried. This notebook contained the transcripts of his conversations with his father, Rav Yehuda Leib Halevi Ashlag (Baal HaSulam), author of the *Sulam* (Ladder) commentary on *The Book of Zohar*, *The Study of the Ten Sefirot* (a commentary on the texts of the Kabbalist, Ari), and of many other works on Kabbalah.

Not feeling well on the Jewish New Year's Eve of September 1991, the Rabash summoned me to his bedside and handed me a notebook, whose cover contained only one word, *Shamati* (I Heard). As he handed the notebook, he said, "Take it and learn from it." The following morning, my teacher perished in my arms, leaving me and many of his other disciples without guidance in this world.

Committed to Rabash's legacy to disseminate the wisdom of Kabbalah, I published the notebook just as it was written, thus retaining the text's transforming powers. Among all the books of Kabbalah, *Shamati* is a unique and compelling creation.

Kabbalah for the Student

Kabbalah for the Student offers authentic texts by Rav Yehuda Ashlag, author of the *Sulam* (Ladder) commentary on *The Book of Zohar*, his son and successor, Rav Baruch Ashlag, as well as other great Kabbalists. It also offers illustrations that accurately depict the evolution of the Upper Worlds as Kabbalists experience them. The book also contains several explanatory essays that help us understand the texts within.

In *Kabbalah for the Student*, Rav Michael Laitman, PhD, Rav Baruch Ashlag's personal assistant and prime student, compiled all the texts a Kabbalah student would need in order to attain the spiritual worlds. In his daily lessons, Rav Laitman bases his teaching on these inspiring texts, thus helping novices and veterans alike to better understand the spiritual path we undertake on our fascinating journey to the Higher Realms.

ABOUT BNEI BARUCH

B nei Baruch is a group of Kabbalists in Israel, sharing the wisdom of Kabbalah with the entire world. Study materials in over 30 languages are based on authentic Kabbalah texts that were passed down from generation to generation.

HISTORY AND ORIGIN

In 1991, following the passing of his teacher, Rav Baruch Shalom HaLevi Ashlag (The Rabash), Rav Michael Laitman, Professor of Ontology and the Theory of Knowledge, PhD in Philosophy and Kabbalah, and MSc in Medical Bio-Cybernetics, established a Kabbalah study group called "Bnei Baruch." He called it Bnei Baruch (Sons of Baruch) to commemorate his mentor, whose side he never left in the final twelve years of his life, from 1979 to 1991. Rav Laitman had been Ashlag's prime student and personal assistant, and is recognized as the successor of Rabash's teaching method.

The Rabash was the firstborn son and successor of Rav Yehuda Leib HaLevi Ashlag, the greatest Kabbalist of the 20th century. Rabbi Ashlag authored the most authoritative and comprehensive commentary on *The Book of Zohar*, titled *The Sulam* (Ladder) *Commentary*. He was the first to reveal the complete method for spiritual ascent, and thus was known as Baal HaSulam (Owner of the Ladder).

Today, Bnei Baruch bases its entire study method on the path paved by these two great spiritual leaders.

THE STUDY METHOD

The unique study method developed by Baal HaSulam and his son, the Rabash, is taught and applied on a daily basis by Bnei Baruch. This method relies on authentic Kabbalah sources such as *The Book of Zohar*, by Rabbi Shimon Bar-Yochai, *The Tree of Life*, by the Holy Ari, and *The Study of the Ten Sefirot*, by Baal HaSulam.

While the study relies on authentic Kabbalah sources, it is carried out in simple language and uses a scientific, contemporary approach. Developing this approach has made Bnei Baruch an internationally respected organization, both in Israel and in the world at large.

The unique combination of an academic study method and personal experiences broadens the students' perspective and awards them a new perception of the reality they live in. Those on the spiritual path are thus given the necessary tools to study themselves and their surrounding reality.

THE MESSAGE

Bnei Baruch is a diverse movement of tens of thousands of students worldwide. Students can choose their own paths and the personal intensity of their studies, according to their unique conditions and abilities. The essence of the message disseminated by Bnei Baruch is universal: unity of the people, unity of nations and love of man.

For millennia, Kabbalists have been teaching that love of man should be the foundation of all human relations. This love prevailed in the days of Abraham, Moses, and the group of Kabbalists that they established. If we make room for these seasoned, yet contemporary values, we will discover that we possess the power to put differences aside and unite.

The wisdom of Kabbalah, hidden for millennia, has been waiting for the time when we would be sufficiently developed and ready to implement its message. Now, it is emerging as a solution that can unite diverse factions everywhere, enabling us, as individuals and as a society, to meet today's challenges.

ACTIVITIES

Bnei Baruch was established on the premise that "only by expansion of the wisdom of Kabbalah to the public can we be awarded complete redemption" (Baal HaSulam).

Therefore, Bnei Baruch offers a variety of ways for people to explore and discover the purpose of their lives, providing careful guidance for beginners and advanced students alike.

KABBALAH TELEVISION

Bnei Baruch established a production company, ARI Films (**www.arifilms.tv**) specializing in production of educational TV programs throughout the world, and in many languages.

In Israel, Bnei Baruch established its own channel, aired through cable and satellite 24/7. The channel is also aired on the Internet at **www.kab.tv**. All broadcasts on the channel are free of charge. Programs are adapted for all levels, from complete beginners to the most advanced.

Additionally, ARI Films produces educational series and documentaries.

INTERNET WEBSITE

Bnei Baruch's international website, **www.kab.info**, presents the authentic wisdom of Kabbalah using essays, books, and original texts. It is by far the most expansive source of authentic Kabbalah material on the net, containing a unique, extensive library for readers to thoroughly explore the wisdom of Kabbalah. Additionally, the media archive, **www.kabbalahmedia.info**, contains more than 5,000 media items, downloadable books, and a vast reservoir of texts, video and audio files in many languages.

Bnei Baruch's online Learning Center offers unique, free Kabbalah lessons for beginners, initiating students into this profound body of knowledge in the comfort of their own homes.

Rav Laitman's daily lessons are also aired live on **www.kab.tv**, along with complementary texts and diagrams.

All these services are provided free of charge.

PAPER

Kabbalah Today is a free monthly paper produced and disseminated by Bnei Baruch in many languages, including English, Hebrew, Spanish, and Russian. It is apolitical, non-commercial, and written in a clear, contemporary style. The purpose of *Kabbalah Today* is to expose the vast knowledge hidden in the wisdom of Kabbalah at no cost and in a clear, engaging format and style for readers everywhere.

Kabbalah Today is distributed free in every major U.S. city, as well as in Toronto, Canada, London, England, and Sydney, Australia. It is printed in English, Hebrew, and Russian, and is also available on the Internet, at **www.kabtoday.com**.

Additionally, a hard copy of the paper is sent to subscribers at delivery cost only.

KABBALAH BOOKS

Bnei Baruch publishes authentic books, written by Rav Yehuda Ashlag (Baal HaSulam), his son, Rav Baruch Ashlag (the Rabash), and Rav Michael Laitman. The books of Rav Ashlag and Rabash are essential for complete understanding of the teachings of authentic Kabbalah, explained in Rav Laitman's lessons.

Rav Laitman writes his books in a clear, contemporary style based on the key concepts of Baal HaSulam. These books are a vital link between today's readers and the original texts. All the books are available for sale, as well as for free download.

KABBALAH LESSONS

As Kabbalists have been doing for centuries, Rav Laitman gives a daily lesson at the Bnei Baruch center in Israel between 3:00‑6:00 a.m. Israel time. The lessons are given in Hebrew and are simultaneously translated into seven languages: English, Russian, Spanish, French, German, Italian, and Turkish. As with everything else, the live broadcast is provided gratis to thousands of students worldwide.

FUNDING

Bnei Baruch is a non-profit organization for teaching and sharing the wisdom of Kabbalah. To maintain its independence and purity of intentions, Bnei Baruch is not supported, funded, or otherwise tied to any government or political organization.

Since the bulk of its activity is provided free of charge, the prime sources of funding for the group's activities are donations and tithing—contributed by students on a voluntary basis—and Rav Laitman's books, which are sold at cost.

HOW TO CONTACT BNEI BARUCH

1057 Steeles Avenue West, Suite 532
Toronto, ON, M2R 3X1
Canada

Bnei Baruch USA,
2009 85th street, #51,
Brooklyn, NY 11214,
USA

E-mail: info@kabbalah.info
Web site: www.kab.info

Toll free in USA and Canada:
1-866-LAITMAN
Fax: 1-905 886 9697